CITIZEN 21

CITIZEN 21

CITIZENSHIP IN THE NEW MILLENNIUM

Compiled by

David Alton

HarperCollins*Publishers*

HarperCollins*Publishers*
77–85 Fulham Palace Road, London W6 8JB
www.**fire**and**water**.com

First published in Great Britain in 2001
by HarperCollins*Publishers*

CONTENTS

FOREWORD

by Frances Lawrence

On a December afternoon, as my four children lit candles to celebrate the joy of Christmas, their father was murdered on a London street. During the four-week trial of his murderer in the Old Bailey, the scenario unfolding before me was witness to Yeats' vision:

> Things fall apart; the centre cannot hold;
> Mere anarchy is loosed upon the world,
> The blood-dimmed tide is loosed, and everywhere
> The ceremony of innocence is drowned...
>
> 'The Second Coming', 1919

In those terrible days, I saw the deeply ingrained shadows at the precipice of society. I learned that they derived inescapably from the dark, fluctuating morality at its core.

When the trial ended, I was asked for my thoughts and I wrote a piece for *The Times* in which I discussed the rise of moral relativism and the *laissez-faire* doctrine which holds that society is best served by the uninhibited pursuit of self-interest. I received literally thousands of letters of support from people who perceived that, in placing an exaggerated emphasis on the desires of the individual and disregarding or denigrating the notion of ourselves as citizens, we were threatening the heart of society.

There is something strangely equivocal about the nature of good citizenship: its principles, so fundamental to our wellbeing, are not innate. They have to be learnt, preferably when young. The consequence of not learning may have, as for my family, dramatic and dreadful implications.

It is never easy, perhaps, to be young, and it seems to me that this is a particularly bewildering time in which people earning vast, disproportionate sums of money are held up as role models. Materialism has become the new theatre, and individualism the dominant ethic. The values which make up a healthy society have gone out of style.

Some children are able to learn these values in the security of their own families. The family, after all, is their first experience of a social group. Within it they enjoy the most basic human rights, at the same time learning that with those rights come responsibilities. Far from being onerous, however, these responsibilities delight them. They learn that there is great pleasure and fulfilment in the giving of help and time and love. They learn that we are individuals with separate destinies – but that we also have an intense desire to belong. It is in belonging and in participating that we best express our common humanity.

There are other children, however, who have become separated from childhood. Physical or spiritual poverty – sometimes both – has undermined their innocence. Devoid of the natural education of a loving family, they inhabit a twilight world in which they learn morally dubious paradigms and yearn for the false camaraderie of a street gang or the empty status symbols of material success. Not having been taught the value of other people, they look only at themselves, seeking fulfilment in their own, private worlds. They are unable to interact positively with other people because this is not something that has occurred within their own life. They are lost souls, confirming the paradox that, although society would not exist without individuals, those individuals exist fully only when they recognize that they are part of society.

People can hardly be expected to take an interest in their community if it is something apart from them, in which they have no stake. They certainly cannot be expected to take an interest in politics if they do not know what they are. They must feel that their voices will be heard – for those without listeners soon lose their voices.

In my article, I argued for citizenship to be learnt in school and so I was delighted when I first heard about the formation of the Advisory Group on Education for Citizenship and the Teaching of Democracy in Schools. I have been concerned, though, at what appears to be a theoretical bias to the proposals. As David Alton says in his introduction, there is no point at all in educating for citizenship if it remains solely as a theory – the old 'civics' lessons of the past – and is never put into practice.

For some people, the idea of educating for citizenship will require a leap of faith, a moving away from the perception that the only measure of successful education is academic success. Of course it is important, but, equally, our job as teachers is to guide our pupils to success in the personal, spiritual and social aspects of their lives.

Citizenship must not be a lesson tacked on to the end of the timetable – but this does not mean that more time is taken up in the curriculum. Educating for citizenship should inform the curriculum in all subjects at all levels when Schemes of Work are being set. We must not only ask the question, 'What are students going to learn here?' but also, 'Through this subject learning, how are we educating for citizenship, for the development of this student as a rounded individual who values and is valued by society?' Further, it has to be planned as a cross-curricular activity in which young people are given an understanding of the history, culture and social and economic development of their community, and are inspired to become constructive members of it. They should be encouraged to interpret the notion of community widely by gaining familiarity with the political context and its national, European and global implications.

The terms 'citizenship' and 'good citizenship' are often used interchangeably. I do not think it matters. An understanding of the former should lead to a realization of the importance of the latter. The practice of the latter may lead to an understanding of the former. What really matters is that educating for citizenship has a dynamism that can shake the core of the school, challenge its teachers and touch the soul of every pupil. Citizenship is best taught by being lived. Otherwise, its meaning will remain for its students as dry words on paper – to be shredded into dust if more convenient.

As seasoned adults we are often disenchanted, sometimes cynical about things that cannot be seen or precisely measured. I agree with David Blunkett who, in his lecture, declared that cynics 'erode every opportunity of changing the world'. Sneering at something provides a refuge from having to face up to it. Instead, I believe it is the duty of us all to rekindle, in our homes, in our schools, in our parishes and in government, the flame of social responsibility.

When I wrote my article, David Alton told me that in his city of Liverpool the heinous murder of James Bulger had a similarly cathartic effect in forcing open a debate about the often violent nature of life. He told me of the work which was under way at the Liverpool John Moores University in developing awards in good citizenship and in cultivating debate about communal duties and personal responsibilities. I particularly welcomed the public lecture series which was proposed.

Three years later I am delighted to see the text of these lectures. I hope that this will be the first volume of several such collections and that they will become a significant resource for teachers grappling with citizenship education, for academic institutions and individuals, for local councillors and people working in voluntary and community organizations, for people in the media and for the general public.

The vicious irony of my husband's death still hammers at my heart. If I had not known it before, I know now that the only true measurement of society is the way its individuals treat one another. Being a good citizen is not a spectator sport or someone else's concern. A healthy, happy society requires each one of us to be its trustee. My hope is that on reading these lectures you will feel encouraged to promote the values of good citizenship, so that this new millennium will be clothed not in stark indifference but in the warmth of our shared humanity.

INTRODUCTION

by David Alton

The Government has announced that all secondary schools will be expected to teach citizenship as part of the national curriculum. Beyond this narrow objective, a more extensive debate has been under way about the relationship between a citizen's rights and duties, and about the chemistry of good citizenship which enables communities to operate successfully.

The unique collection of lectures published here attempts to address some of these issues and to open a debate about what we mean by citizenship. The lectures were staged in Liverpool over the past three years by the Liverpool John Moores University's Foundation for Citizenship, and the organizers have been genuinely surprised by the substantial uptake of tickets by the general public. In an age when we are told that public lectures and meetings are old hat, up to 800 people have been crowding into civic venues to listen and then to participate in a lively exchange of opinions. It is not an exaggeration to say that this exercise has, in itself, been a significant contribution to the rebuilding of a civil society in a city where normal democratic exchange had been substantially diminished by a period of chaotic government.

Sponsored by Granada Television, who recorded the lectures, thus enabling JMU students to turn them into videos which have been made available to schools and the wider public, the lectures clearly have a greater national importance beyond the Mersey-side audiences who originally heard them. I am, therefore, indebted to HarperCollins for enabling their publication in this collection.

Before you begin to read the individual contributions, let me offer a word of caution about the way in which we are intending to educate for citizenship. I passionately believe that it is part of the task of education to prepare children to take up their duties and responsibilities in society. Nevertheless, if this is done by turning citizenship into yet another subject to be evaluated and assessed by everyone from head teachers to OFSTED, it is likely to have a counterproductive effect. Some of us will remember the valiant attempts to teach British Constitution and Civics – and the marginal interest which they attracted.

Let me list my principal concerns clearly:

1 What is the rationale in making citizenship a mandatory subject in secondary schools but not in primary schools?
2 How are teachers to be prepared for the task of teaching citizenship?
3 What resources are to be made available to schools?
4 Is this to be portrayed as just another academic subject, liable to end up overloading the national curriculum and, even more disastrously, subject to examination?
5 Is there a covert agenda to replace religious education with secular citizenship?
6 What is the purpose of citizenship education?

The Government has decided to introduce citizenship education following a report drawn up by Professor Bernard Crick, a former tutor of the Education Secretary, David Blunkett. Many of Crick's impulses are good, but the final recommendations are sometimes fuzzy. The decision to concentrate on citizenship education in the secondary sector is an example of this. Primary schools are particularly good at developing cross-curriculum themes, and citizenship lends itself especially well to this approach. There is also a lot of truth in the old adage, 'Give me a child until he or she is seven and I will give you a man or woman for life.'

I visited some primary schools in Warrington last year. They used William Golding's story of *Lord of the Flies* during their literacy hour. The children were put into small groups and asked to imagine that, like Golding's children, they had been marooned on a desert island. What would they do? The children then learnt the art of negotiation and discussion. Unsurprisingly, when they came to report their findings, the rapporteurs listed their priorities as making rules and providing shelter and protection for the younger children. I used to have a poster on my office wall that said, 'God so loved the world that he didn't send a committee,' but anyone who wants to take part in any activities related to citizenship needs to learn the art of working through committees. That is what these children were doing.

In the secondary sector there are plenty of opportunities while teaching English, history, geography, economics and the sciences to explore questions relating to the obligations of a citizen – not least issues of personal responsibility and good ethics. This can be done without making citizenship a component of the national curriculum, although there should probably be a mandatory requirement on schools to decide how best to promote good citizenship through their existing curriculum arrangements.

I recently spoke at the national conference of teachers who work in some of our church-run schools, and also to a conference of Merseyside head teachers. At both gatherings I was told about anxieties concerning curriculum overload and being given yet another responsibility to discharge without proper training or adequate resources. Why do we never listen to the professional teachers before introducing more changes? Happily, organizations such as Community Service Volunteers are beginning to provide some teaching resources, but there is a desperate need for more. It is an ideal opportunity to use new technologies and to provide an interactive website and CD-ROMS exploring citizenship questions. I should like to see great historical issues such as the Holocaust, slavery and the Irish Famine used as an entry point to teach young citizens about contemporary questions of anti-Semitism, racism, modern slavery and present-day famine, and about what they can do as individuals – everything from how to write a letter to a newspaper or an MP, to how to join voluntary organizations or pressure groups.

There is a quiet lobby which – behind the scenes – has said that it would like to jettison religious education and put citizenship studies in its place. The present Prime Minister and his Secretary of State for Education would oppose this, but it is as well to be aware that this is the agenda which some would like to pursue. It betrays their own lack of understanding of religion in society and an intolerance of cultural and religious diversity.

Finally, citizenship needs to be experienced rather more than taught. On Merseyside, the Citizenship Award scheme which I have developed with Liverpool John Moores University now operates in all 600 primary and secondary schools. The awards are sponsored by local and national companies. The school recognizes the existing achievements of young people who are already acting as good citizens – striving to be men and women for others. The local newspaper, the *Liverpool Echo*, tells their stories and each child receives a university certificate to keep in their record of achievement. The concept has been exported elsewhere and Rochdale, for instance, now operates the same scheme, in conjunction with Salford University.

Our award programme has been backed up by the 'town and gown' public lecture series reproduced in this book. The lectures have been delivered by figures as diverse as the President of Ireland, the Home Secretary and the Shadow Home Secretary, Baroness Williams of Crosby, the Education Secretary, the Archbishops of Canterbury and Birmingham, the Chief Rabbi, and leading figures from the media. At the beginning of each lecture some of the recipients of the citizenship awards have been recognized publicly.

The lectures have been named for William Roscoe, who was briefly a Member of Parliament. In 1807 he risked the wrath of his constituents by supporting William Wilberforce in the anti-slavery lobby, stating that there was a Higher Judge before whom he and the citizens of a city which made its wealth from the ownership of slaves would one day have to stand. Roscoe subsequently devoted his life to campaigning against slavery, supporting the arts, and establishing educational institutions (one of which is the progenitor of today's flourishing John Moores University). As Magnus Magnusson reminded us in his lecture, Roscoe was also an early environmentalist.

For my money, a less dirigiste approach to citizenship would be in order. In Britain we managed to turn 'community service' into a punishment to be dispensed by magistrates. It would be a pity if we now turned 'citizenship' into a lesson which pupils came to regard either as a burden or as a waste of time.

EDUCATING FOR CITIZENSHIP

Stephen Dorrell

12 NOVEMBER 1997

The Rt Hon. Stephen Dorrell MP is the Conservative Member of Parliament for Charnwood. He was formerly the Secretary of State for Health.

The British came late to the concept of citizenship. In many continental countries, as well as in the United States, political and constitutional development involved formal statements of individual rights and constitutional process. The rights of the citizen were formally linked to a responsibility for safeguarding them. The English common law tradition discourages this whole approach. Our constitutional development has proceeded almost entirely without formal statements either of individual rights or of constitutional process. A British subject was thought to need no formal statement of his or her rights. He or she was assumed to be free to act according to his or her own will, unless it could be shown that either common law or statute established a prohibition.

This common law approach recognized implicitly a characteristic of successful free societies which today's world requires us to make explicit. By avoiding formal statements of rights and focusing on a scheme of duties, the common lawyer's approach avoids the danger of an overconcentration on rights and entitlements and recognizes that acceptance of a duty is the essential precondition to the creation of a right.

One of the hallowed texts of the post-war Conservative Party is the 'One Nation' pamphlet published by a group of Conservative MPs in October 1950. The 'One Nation' slogan has, of course, recently won wider endorsement, but that pamphlet recognized the need to make the link between rights and responsibilities explicit. It stated:

> The existence of a nation depends on the steady and indeed distinctive acceptance by those who compose it of a scheme of duties. It may also imply a scheme of rights; but the health and life of the nation are endangered as soon as the rights come to be regarded as more important than the duties, or even their prior condition.

Lady Thatcher famously put it rather differently when she declared in an interview, 'There is no such thing as society.' It may have been an occasion when her instinct for a soundbite got the better of her natural caution, but her argument was in truth exactly the same, as she went on to make clear: 'There are many individual men and women, and there are families. No government can do anything except through people: people must look to themselves first. It's our duty to look after ourselves and then also to look after our neighbour. People have got entitlements too much in mind without the obligations. There is no such thing as an entitlement unless someone has first met an obligation.'

That is the core of the concept of citizenship. A free society does not exist as an abstract entity, independent of the people who live within it. It comes into existence when a group of individuals choose to bind themselves together with ties of mutual right and obligation, and it is those ties which are the foundation of citizenship – as they are the foundation of freedom itself.

Freedom and citizenship are children of the same parents. Edmund Burke understood that very well – although contemporary experience in France discouraged him from using the word 'citizen'. He spoke instead of what he called 'social freedom'. Writing to a friend in Paris at the end of 1789, Burke said:

> Permit me to tell you what the freedom is that I love, and that to which I think all men intitled [sic]. It is not solitary, unconnected, individual, selfish Liberty. As if every Man was to regulate the whole of his Conduct by his own will. The Liberty I mean is Social Freedom. It is that state of things in which Liberty is secured by the equality of Restraints; a Constitution of things in which the liberty of no one Man, and no body of Men, and no number of Men can find Means to trespass on the Liberty of any Person or description of Persons in the Society. This kind of Liberty is indeed but another name for Justice, ascertained by wise laws and secured by well-constructed institutions. I am sure that Liberty, so incorporated, and in a manner identified with justice, must be infinitely dear to everyone who is capable of conceiving what it is. But whenever a separation is made between Liberty and Justice, neither is, in my opinion, safe.

Burke's vision still seems direct and fresh over 200 years after it was written. It sets out the nature of the relationship between the citizens of a free society.

He begins with the rule of law, for without law civil society cannot exist. Stalin's Soviet system accorded rights to everyone, but he fooled only the gullible because he provided no framework of law which allowed the citizen to enforce those rights. Lawyers can sometimes be tendentious and frustrating people, but they are the indispensable sentinels of freedom.

Burke goes on to stress the importance of controlling the influence of powerful interests within society who would otherwise 'trespass' on the liberties of other citizens. He probably had in mind the directors of the East India Company. That threat has passed, but the need to ensure that the interests of the citizen are protected from abuse by the powerful certainly has not.

Perhaps the most striking thought contained in this passage of Burke's writing is the importance he places on protecting the interests of minorities. We have become familiar with the concept of rule by majority, but Burke makes it clear that he remains concerned about the interests of the citizen as an individual, even when he or she is in a minority. His own experience as an Irish Catholic living in England would have ensured that he fully understood the need to integrate modern ethnic minorities fully into our society.

Another point which Burke makes explicit is the link between liberty and justice. 'Whenever a separation is made between Liberty and Justice,' he writes, 'neither is, in my opinion, safe.' Different generations will, of course, have different views about what constitutes justice, but an arid attempt to define the rights and duties of citizenship without taking account of contemporary views of justice is doomed to fail.

Finally, and most importantly, Burke is dismissive of what he calls 'solitary, unconnected, individual, selfish Liberty'. 'The Liberty I mean,' he writes, 'is Social Freedom.' Freedom and citizenship are inextricably linked together because the full development of the citizen can only take place within a free and ordered society. To talk of freedom only in terms of rights is meaningless. Liberty without responsibility is mere licence.

How, then, do we 'educate for citizenship'? Not, surely, by a sterile discussion about political institutions. The society I have been describing will certainly have an active political life, but the overwhelming majority of its citizens will go about their lives without believing themselves to be engaged on a political enterprise. To reduce (and 'reduce' is the right word) the great majority of the rights and obligations which the individual citizen feels are personal or local to the language of politics is to demean them.

A proper understanding of the meaning of citizenship begins with our natural feelings towards members of our own family. For most of us, the responsibility of the parent for the young child is no more than a basic human instinct. It is so obvious that it does not need restating. But is that the end of family obligation? Surely not. The modern concept of a nuclear family has become hopelessly narrow and debilitating. If we look outside our own culture and, indeed, if we look to our own history, we will find a much richer tradition on which to draw.

The bonds of family should not be limited to the parents' responsibility for their young children. It also involves the grown-up children's responsibility for their parents in old age. It involves the support which grandparents can give when their own children become parents in their turn. It involves the continuing ties between brother and sister, and the extended network of support that can be available from uncles, aunts, nephews and nieces.

When I was an unmarried man in my twenties, I was asked at a Conservative candidate selection meeting, 'Mr Dorrell, are you married, and do you have a family?'

My answer caused a flutter among the assembled Conservative ladies: 'The answer to the first question is "no"; to the second it is "yes".'

It may have caused a flutter, but I remain convinced that it was the right answer. We all have family ties, and a proper understanding of citizenship should recognize this.

There are, of course, many pressures in the modern world which are changing the nature of these relationships, and they cannot all be dismissed as social degeneration. Labour mobility, for example, is something which we all tend, rightly, to regard as desirable when we are discussing economic policy. But labour mobility that takes a young couple away from their parents undermines the capacity both of the family to support the couple in raising their own family, and of the couple in later life to support their parents in old age. Similarly, and sometimes more controversially, improved economic opportunities for women inevitably place new strains on family relationships, both within and beyond the nuclear family, particularly when – as will increasingly be the case – women are geographically mobile independently of their partners.

Few of us would regard the implications of these changes as sufficient reason to prevent ambitious people from pursuing improved opportunity. It is one of the most attractive character-istics of the modern world that our society has become more open and mobile, and that individuals have opportunities to pursue their interests and talents in a way that earlier genera-tions simply never dreamt was possible. To turn our backs on those improved opportunities for fulfilment is neither necessary nor desirable. But we clearly do need to think more seriously than we have yet been willing to do about the implications of these changes for the scheme of rights and duties which we understand by the concept of a family, and which I believe are the bedrock on which a proper understanding of the concept of citizenship is built.

Family is only one aspect of citizenship, however. We all have ties of personal obligation with neighbours and friends within our locality which come together to create another important aspect of the life of a citizen. 'Community' is a word which is more often used than understood, but it forms an essential part of citizenship. It is the basis of the sense of commitment which is felt by the great majority of us towards the locality in which we live. That commitment leads people to involve themselves in a wide range of voluntary activity, contributing to the community through social work, concern about the environment, church activity, care for local landmarks or service on local authorities or as school governors. About half of all adults in Britain take part in organized voluntary work – a vast army of volunteers who demonstrate by their actions their commitment to a sense of citizenship.

These allegiances are of huge importance. They give us all a sense of belonging, a sense of our own importance. They provide a framework for our lives which is rooted in local people, local history and local tradition. Our ties of affinity are not to units of administration, they are to people, places, land-marks, institutions and customs. It is those local allegiances which give our society human scale as well as real diversity. They create pride and self-confidence.

Liverpool, like many other big cities in Britain, has seen a resurgence in its self-confidence in recent years. It is a city with a proud history and a sharp sense of its own identity. Different citizens will identify with different aspects of the life of the city, whether with its two cathedrals, its two football clubs or the Liverpool Philharmonic. All of them express the spirit of the city. Imagine Liverpool without any one of them. It is not simply that life would be impoverished: the structure of life in the city would be weakened because the capacity of its citizens to articu-late civic pride and civic identity would be diminished. Local allegiances give our society tangible roots as well as shape and purpose. They underwrite its stability. They are the antithesis of George Orwell's *Nineteen Eighty-Four*, where individuality and diversity were pulverized in the service of political abstractions.

It is only against the background of these personal and local ties that our sense of national identity can be properly under-stood. Patriotism is a much abused concept, but it forms an essential part of our sense of who we are. It is the means by which we relate to the outside world, as well as to those who came before and those who will come after. Strong national institutions are the means by which the achievements of one generation benefit later generations. We should never forget that we inherited freedom itself as a result of the sacrifice and vigilance of earlier generations of our countrymen. Along with freedom, we inherited the institutions which safeguard it – a mature democracy, the rule of law, a strong public service ethic, disciplined armed forces and a sense of justice and fair play.

Furthermore, the accumulated experience of the nation runs much wider than that. Every day British industry trades around the world as a result of contacts and friendships built up over generations. Our children are educated and the sick are treated in institutions which draw strength from their history. We inherited a legacy in music, literature and the visual arts which conveys a powerful sense of what it means to be British.

The benefits of British citizenship pervade every aspect of our lives. Our inheritance should engender in us a consciousness not of the rights of ownership, but of the duties of trusteeship. We should use our inheritance for the service of this generation; we should allow it to evolve where necessary; we should judge harshly those who prejudice it or seek to exploit it for their own selfish ends; and we should commit ourselves to pass it on, enriched, to our children. That is what educating for citizenship is about. Citizenship is not a discrete subject, to be practised in a single compartment of our lives. We are social animals; our actions create the environment in which we and our neighbours live and which our children inherit. It is through understanding the nature of those relationships that we understand the nature of citizenship.

It is sometimes surprising how unattractive freedom can sound. Lectures about liberty and citizenship always stress the importance of responsibility and obligation, and I have set out the reasons why I believe it is important that they do. As a French countess remarked on her way to the guillotine, 'Freedom. Freedom. What crimes are committed in thy name.'

The responsible free society is not only about burdens and obligations, however. It is also about opportunity. It gives its citizens the opportunity to enjoy their own talents and to make their own way in the world. It seeks to enlarge the field of individual endeavour. It creates ladders for people to climb and it rewards those who climb them, both to mark their individual achievement and to encourage others to emulate their example.

It is the diversity of the successful free society which is its chief glory. It is open, unpredictable and disputatious. It does not seek conformity – indeed, the very thought repels it. It celebrates the successes of its citizens and revels in their variety. It is truly one nation – not because all its citizens are the same, but because they all feel themselves to be playing a part in the same endeavour.

MAKING THE DIFFERENCE: AN INDEPENDENT VIEW

Martin Bell

29 JANUARY 1998

Martin Bell MP is the Independent Member of Parliament for Tatton. He was formerly the BBC Foreign Affairs Correspondent.

I am the eighth largest parliamentary party (the ninth largest if you include Sinn Féin, which has not taken its seats) – party leader, rank and file, chief whip. What you see is what you get. The first party conference of the season is my conference. It is held in a tent at Mere in the Tatton constituency. It is all party and no conference. I am not only the smallest parliamentary party, I am also the most united. I have not had a falling-out with myself yet.

Yet I ask myself quite often, 'Why did I do it?' Every day of that campaign, my daughter Melissa, who is much more savvy politically than I am, said, 'Dad, what have you got us into and why have you got us into it?' I could not often give a very good answer. Then, driving up last Friday for yet another political life-or-death news conference in Knutsford, I thought to myself, 'How am I going to handle this?' And then I thought, 'The only people who matter are the real people; they're the little people, they're the people often left out of the political equation or taken for granted by their political leaders.' So I said to myself, 'I know what I'll do. I'll throw myself on the mercy of the people.' This is a very audacious, if not stupid, thing for an MP to do, because you can invite yourself to a 'write-in' vote by your opponents. I told them that if I had lost their confidence, or if I still had their confidence, they should write and tell me. They wrote and, as of this morning, I have had 700 letters in favour and seven against, so it's going OK.

Yet I did ask myself as I drove up that day, 'Is it worth it?' Campaigning, as all politicians know, can be pretty brutal. It is especially brutal if you are somewhat isolated, alone, exposed, expected to deliver miracles and you wear a white suit. People tend to have expectations of you which an ordinary politician cannot deliver, and I am a flawed, frail human being. I make mistakes and sometimes I tell my people I was wrong. Sometimes I will say, 'I've changed my mind.' I have also told them something they very seldom hear, which is that I have no political ambitions and I am going to stand for one term only and that is going to be that.

Then I ask myself, really, 'Why do I put myself through this when I could be cruising to the end of a very satisfying BBC career?' (I would have been retired in August of this year.) The answer actually lies in the shining eyes of the children. There was something about that extraordinary episode which fired up the kids and made them aware that politics is for them as well. I did not intend to do it; I had no pollster, no strategist; it just happened. It caught fire and it started, amazingly, in the primary schools. Ten- and 11-year-olds would come into my little head-quarters and deliver poems or drawings they had done the night before. They would pick up little lapel badges and they would go home and canvas their parents, and, my word, it worked (though I was later told that Joseph Stalin had done much the same thing). It was really inspiring.

I have since been asked to head a campaign by UNICEF, the UN Children's Fund, for the protection of children in conflict. I cannot say no to that. They also asked me to hold a series of 11 children's surgeries around the country. This arises from the UN Convention on the Rights of the Child. While the rights of the child do not include the right to vote, they do include the right to be listened to, and we think we are going to extend this round the country – I hope next year in every constituency. Perhaps Granada Television could use their House of Commons set for a televised version of this. I think it would make wonderful television. Think about it.

After this session, amazingly, the kids gave me three cheers. I do not know why they did it, but afterwards I got a call from one of the teachers who said, 'I don't know why they do it, but one of them said you're like the sixth Spice Girl.'

'What kind of spice should I be?' I asked.

The answer came back, quick as a flash, 'Old Spice, of course.'

So why *did* I do it? The other thing I told the kids (and I think this is the heart of it; I think this is why they rather warm to the idea of a Citizen MP) was that, if I can be an MP, anybody can be an MP. It takes no special political skills, but it does take a determination to serve other people besides yourself, and it takes a belief that you can make a difference.

Long before my political accident, when I came out of Bosnia, I felt that, if I had lived through this ordeal, I must be able to learn from it and connect other people to the lessons that I thought had to be learnt. I did two school prize-givings a year (otherwise it was getting out of hand). I had a standard speech and at every prize-giving it was well received by the kids, because I was the only being standing between them and their summer holidays and my speech was shorter than that of any other prize-giver.

I remember how these individuals – usually middle-aged politicians, often superannuated, often members of the House of Lords – would come before us and go on for ever. The years rolled by, and suddenly I am that man in the suit – but I spoke very briefly and I would always end like this: 'But from where I have been and what I have seen in the world, there are a few things I wish you to know. One is that good and evil are not abstractions but active forces. Another is that the old adage holds true that, for evil to prosper, all that is necessary is for good people to do nothing. Another is that here, in this or any other part of this kingdom, we live in a blessed and peaceful corner of a turbulent world.'

Most of all, the lesson I tried to impress on them was that, in this unpredictable, and (as I know to my cost) in some ways more dangerous world than the predictable world of the Cold War in which my generation grew up, the difference that individuals can make is so much greater. When, in early April, I was unexpectedly asked to be a kind of apprentice politician, something I never even dreamt of for myself, the first protective instinct was to say, 'No, I'm not going to do that. Politics is for politicians.' Well, politics is *not* for politicians – politics is for people. I think I took it on because I had long believed that the individual can make a difference, and here I was, being asked to make a difference.

Had I walked away, I know I would have regretted it for the rest of my days. I know the regrets that I have are not for the things that I did do, they are for the things I did not do – the challenge not taken, the road not gone down, and I will always wonder till the end of my days if I could have done something better, something more, made the world a little less worse if I had gone down that particular road. So I decided to have a go on the basis of trying to make a difference. I was not the first one they approached, incidentally. I know they approached my good friend Terry Waite, who was much better qualified for the task than I was because he actually comes from the constituency (his mother comes from Styal, near Wilmslow). He turned it down on a wonderful argument, however: he said he had already done one five-year term as a hostage and he did not want to do another.

It is possible for an individual to make a difference. One such is Colonel Mark Cook, the first commander of British troops in former Yugoslavia. At that time the British contingent consisted of a field hospital and a few engineers, and he was rightly concerned about the safety of the engineers in Sarajevo. They were putting up sandbags for other people, but they themselves had no protection. I remember complaining about it in a BBC report, at which point the Army solved the problem, not by sending out protection, but by sending out a military spin-doctor to assure me that I had got it all wrong.

I met Mark and found that he was worried about two things. One was the safety of his troops, and the other was a project he had just started in Croatia. He had come upon a pile of rubble, which was all that remained of an orphanage in Lipik with about 70 kids. The kids had been in the cellar – this was on the front line between the Croats and the Serbs – and they had barely escaped with their lives. They were sent off to the coast, and all that was left was this pile of rubble. Mark determined that he was going to rebuild this orphanage. It was not part of his military duties. He and his soldiers worked at clearing the rubble in their spare time. Then they discovered that it would have to be rebuilt in exactly the same old Austro-Hungarian style as the original, and it was going to cost a million pounds.

It was at that point that, instead of throwing up his hands in despair, he came to see me on that day in Sarajevo, as the only person in the media he knew, to say, 'How do I raise that money?'

I told him, 'I don't know how you raise that money – look at the state of my bank account. I'm no good at raising money at all.' At that moment, somebody came with word that there was a street battle going on about a mile away. I said, 'I've got to go and do the business here. Will you come with me? Your job is also to see the dangers in the streets.'

Well, that was the day I got mortared and wounded and carried off. Mark then did an interview on the BBC's one o'clock news about what had happened to me. At the end of this, he was able to put in a plug for the rebuilding of his orphanage and it was from that moment that the thing took off. Mark raised his million pounds, and the orphanage was opened a year and a half later. He is now the leader of a small but highly effective charity called Hope and Homes for Children, which is building or rebuilding orphanages in Sarajevo, Albania and Mozambique. This is what one man has done. He had a distinguished army career, but nothing in it gave him the satisfaction that he got from what he did beyond the call of duty thereafter, helping people, making the world a less worse place – an inspiring example, if you will, of citizenship.

I cannot emulate that. All I can do for the next three or four years is to try, first of all, to stay out of trouble, but I have also got to pick my causes. I have to pick the causes on which I might possibly be effective. If you accept every challenge and every request, you just cannot do it. I turn down 50 speaking invitations a week. I turn down offers to be patron of this and patron of that. You have to concentrate on where you can be effective, and I do not even know if I can do that. It may well be that all I can achieve in politics, I achieved on 1 May – in which case I shall be a footnote, a modestly significant footnote, to the politics of the 1997 Election, but no more than that.

I would like to be a little more than that, and I do not know if it is going to work out or not. However, the kind of issues on which I would hope to be effective are those concerned with involving people, and especially young people, in the process of government. I also want to be querying why, in this new world we live in, there is a new economy, a new politics, in every respect *except* that we still have the same party politics as we had in the last generation, in the generation before that, and all the way back to Gladstone and Disraeli. We must ask ourselves: is this suiting us? When a backbencher has to whisper to me in the smoking room lest he or she be overheard by the whip, I would not say that it is the politics of fear, but it is certainly the politics of extreme caution. I understand why the whipping system is as strong as it is, but I think there should be a possibility for independents to speak out. One who still does is Tam Dalyell. Splendid, eccentric, old Etonian baronet, Labour – he is all of the above, *and* he has been threatened with deselection, a matter on which he is wonderfully well informed. He is one of the few MPs who can cause the chamber to fill up while they are speaking.

I do wonder about the party system. I think, in my own accidental case, that people were voting for more than just an untried apprentice politician against somebody under a little bit of a cloud. I think they were also wondering whether the party system did justice to the situation. I am not attacking party politics. I like the idea of parties. Parties are grouped around principles. Yet every now and again the system does not work, and it was failing to work, not just in the Tatton case but also in other cases towards the end of the last Parliament. There were so many instances of corrupt politicians that there had to be a problem, quite a severe problem. I do not think there was even a lot of corruption in British politics at that time, but even a little corruption is too much and the people will not stand for it. One of the things they were voting for in Tatton was an honest and open process in which influence would not be bought and sold. I think that was important.

My role as an independent, however, was not to replace the party system. I am not challenging the party system. One of the reasons I promised to stand for one term only was that I wanted to reassure people that I was not breaking the mould, I was not starting an independent party. I received a splendid letter from a chap in Ipswich one day. I get letters like this every week, all the time, every day. 'What would be wonderful,' he wrote, 'would be a White Party, a non-party of independents scattered about the chamber like a dusting of dandruff on an absurdly polychromatic parliament, each in a white suit, each there to ask the awkward questions, to keep it honest and hold them to their promises.'

Well, it isn't going to happen. I shall be out of politics as soon as this Parliament is over, and then they can go back to their three-party politics and that will be fine, because I will have served a purpose. There was something wrong in the system. I think it was the downside of the upside of Thatcherism. In the first two terms under Margaret Thatcher the country benefited in some ways: things worked better, there was a shaking down. Yet, because it was so materialistic and because there was no measure of worth but the financial, a lot of people got in there who had, shall we say, a taste for the bubbly stuff and not much else. They desired to serve themselves. There was a lack of principle, and I think what I have done is to purge that. If you consider me a political Alka-Seltzer, then that is as far as we got.

Nonetheless, it worked and now I want to make sure that, as an independent, I make a difference on issues like the funding of political campaigns, when one party can raise £13 million and another £26 million for a national campaign, while the constituency campaigns are held (quite properly) to just a few thousand. Any party that does this can open itself far too easily to accusations of influence buying and selling. Even if the accusations are false, the *appearance* of wrongdoing can be almost as damaging to public trust as any actual wrongdoing. So why not set a £2 million national campaign limit on any party? You can run a pretty effective campaign for £2 million, granted that there is free broadcasting time. You still have your party political broadcasts.

What are you spending the funds on, anyway? Billboards? This is one of the subsidiary campaigns I am getting into. Did you know that the normal standards of truth in advertising which apply in commercial cases do not apply to political parties? They can say what they like about each other and the usual standards do not apply. I am going to work with an organization of British advertisers who think this is bringing not only politics into disrepute but also their own business. We are going to try to change that. Again, I do not know if I can make it work, but, my goodness, I can try.

Another issue is the very confrontational nature of the House of Commons itself. I think it turns people off that the two front benches are just two sword lengths away from each other (that is why it was set out like that). I do not think that can be changed, but I do see a wonderful use for the Dome: it is at least the right shape for a parliament. Somehow I do not think I am going to succeed with that either.

I would like to be effective on some issues of electoral reform, however. Next year we are going to have proportional representation for the European elections, which is fine. The Government is now deciding which system will be used. I was at a meeting of electoral-reform-minded MPs recently (it does not matter what party it was) when an established MEP got up and said that they rather liked what they called the 'closed list system', in which the party presents the voter with a slate of candidates. You cannot choose between them; you cannot pick some candidates from one list and some from another; you are entirely stuck with the party's choice. That has about as much attraction for me as the rule book of the old Bulgarian Communist Party. We should be doing better than this. We should be asking questions, and I think a new Parliament is the time and place to do it. I am going to try to be effective. I may yet end up being totally ineffectual. I do not know, but I shall try.

I have said on a number of occasions that this new life of mine is a bit like the old one in the sense of being a bit of a battlefield. It is not a military battlefield, but it is a political battlefield, and last week, when I was briefly under fire, it was exactly the same feeling as being on the Golan Heights in 1973 or in Sarajevo three years ago and awaiting the incoming artillery. There is really nothing you can do except hope and pray. Yet I think it needs a different kind of courage from battlefield courage. If you are on a battlefield, your first mistake can be your last, and probably will be. Therefore you have to live at a very high level of alertness. You must not be afraid of fear. You are afraid of panic, because panic is what kills you. Fear, however, is what keeps you alive. It tells you to be very careful and to remain alert. This did not apply to the ordinary people of Sarajevo, the little people who always get shafted – in war as in peace – because they were stuck there under siege for three and a half years. By contrast, we journalists were privileged: we had body armour, we had armoured vehicles, we had UN passes, we could come and go as we pleased. We were sometimes under fire, but we were lucky and the little people were not.

I did not need that much courage in the war zone, because I could always get out of it. I think, however, in order to make a difference in Parliament and in politics, especially when everybody is going to be after me (and I know they would love to have me), it is going to require courage of a different order, a tougher courage. To be quite honest, I do not know if I have this – it was failing me a little bit last week – but the wonderful letters I received, including some from Mr Hamilton's former supporters, have rekindled that courage. Many of the slogans, however, were of the *nil carborundum illegitimi* variety, if you get the allusion, and from people who said, 'Don't you dare quit.' If I quit, they would be angry, and some of these almost made me cry.

One little kid sent me a pound towards my legal expenses. I cannot take it, because I paid the money back three days ago from my savings. It is going into a contingency fund in case anyone is fool enough to attack me. I paid it out of my savings because there was a windfall in the Halifax Building Society last year and all the members of the Halifax were polled on whether they wanted to make themselves richer. I was part of the one per cent who said, 'I don't, actually. I want my building society to be a building society and not a bank, and I don't want the directors to be able to award themselves large emoluments.' Well, we lost. So I got this money (I did not actually send it back, I have to say). I salted it away in the Halifax Building Society and I said to myself, 'One day it's going to come in handy.' Well, it did.

I have a set of political beliefs which are fairly inconsistent with the platform of any party – little bits of one and little bits of the other – but I do not think that makes a difference. I think what makes a difference (and this is what I tell the kids) is a fundamental determination to help other people rather than yourself. John Stalker, who is a friend of mine and, as far as I am concerned, is Mr Integrity in the Northwest, came to see me at my lowest point in the campaign. It was the day after the Battle of Knutsford Heath, and he came and asked if he could be of any use to me. I said, 'You bet, John,' and he stayed with me and he is a friend to this day. The endorsements that mattered most to me were those of John Stalker and Alex Ferguson, who gave me the most helpful handshake.

John said something which brings us back to this theme of gaining the confidence of the young and involving the young in the political process. If you think your politicians are on the take, if you think they are serving only themselves, and if indeed they *are* on the take (in one case £20,000 was admitted for taking questions, and that was not the worst case), then what kind of signal does that send to the kids on the estates in Wythenshawe? What kind of signal? I think it is a question of restoring a little bit of respect, and I think this Parliament is beginning to have it. I think it has a different attitude to the last Parliament. There are many fewer consultancies – declared or undeclared. There is a different attitude and I think some MPs are beginning to realize that it just might be possible to live on a salary of £43,000 a year after all. I represent one of the most affluent constituencies in the country, but there are areas of shameful neglect in the overspill estates. You cannot go to people like this and say, 'I can't live on that kind of money.' I hope to make a little bit of an impression on that kind of issue as well.

I want to end up with a few words about kindness and courage, because I think kindness and courage are essentially what politicians need. I did not know Diana, Princess of Wales, very well but I did get to know her through the landmines campaign. I know she once gave a speech at a charity event in Washington at which she quoted from a little poem. It might sound naive. I don't know about that, but it goes to the heart of the matter:

Life is mostly froth and bubble,
Two things stand like stone:
Kindness in another's trouble,
Courage in your own.

Adam Lindsay Gordon, 1866

THE CITIZEN IN THE MODERN WORLD

Shirley Williams

13 FEBRUARY 1998

Baroness Williams of Crosby is the Deputy Leader of the Liberal Democrats in the House of Lords. She was a Labour MP (1964–79), serving in the Cabinet from 1974 to 1979 as Secretary of State for Education and Science and Paymaster-General, and was a co-founder of the Social Democratic Party in 1981. She is Public Service Professor Emeritus at the John F. Kennedy School of Government, Harvard University.

This lecture is like Gaul – it is divided into three parts. The first part is about the concept of citizenship as it has come down to us. The second part is about what modern citizenship constitutes – and I believe there are some extraordinarily profound changes that we have to take on board. The third and final part is about education for citizenship – on which, here at Liverpool John Moores University, you have made such a splendid beginning.

Citizenship is obviously a very deep and old idea. In some ways, over the millennia, we have struggled to get back to the ideal of the Greek republic, an ideal which remained an ideal, but nevertheless was a phenomenal leap for the people of that period before the birth of Christ, the concept of a self-governing *polis*. The fundamental thoughts of the Greeks were best summed up in Cicero's definition of what was civic virtue – i.e. virtue was about actively taking part in the government, about being a fully participative citizen who in every possible way was part of his (yes, just his) republic. Let me quote from Cicero: 'The existence of virtue depends entirely on its use and its noblest use is the government of the State.' Today that sounds a very strange idea.

The Romans saw citizenship in a more passive way. For them the great principle was that government was a government of laws and not of men, a crucial building block in the concept of citizenship. Even today, let us say in respect of the American President or the British Prime Minister, no person is above the law, and all people are bound by the same law. It is a critical concept of democratic citizenship that this should be so. While the Romans had this concept of the rule of law and equal protection by the laws, however, they had much less of an idea of the full involvement of citizens in the government of the State.

Already, early technology was shaping the idea of citizenship. Rome moved from Republic to Empire and became a huge territory in which the democracy of a Democritus or a Pericles was simply no longer possible. At the Agora in Athens, Pericles could address perhaps 10,000 people. The Roman Empire, and even the Republic before it, had to address a much larger audience. This meant that, from personal communication, man to man, there developed bureaucratic communication, officials to citizens, over the whole of the Empire. The crucial fact about Rome, however, was that every citizen of the Republic and later of the Empire was of similar standing and bound by similar laws.

I am now going to skip many centuries in order to bring in three other ideas. The first of those ideas is the concept of the rights of citizens – their right to be heard and their right to be represented. You can sum that up in the pregnant phrase that came out of the American War of Independence: 'No taxation without representation.' It has echoes all the way up to our own time in respect of such matters as the poll tax, which I will talk about later on. 'No taxation without representation' is another of those principles that helps to build the idea of citizenship today.

Then, of course, there was the French Revolution, with its fundamental concept that citizenship is built upon rights, the rights of every citizen. It was what we call 'rights-based' democracy. The French Revolution, however, was in many ways not quite as revolutionary as one might think, and I will come on to that in a while.

Before I do so, let me pay credit to two other contributions that came essentially from the British tradition. The first of those was the concept that government depended upon trust – not coercion, but trust – between the citizens and those who governed them. That was part of the central lesson of John Locke. He talked about a social contract, not in the French sense but in the British sense of understanding that, because men wanted to live in harmony and peace with one another and also wanted to protect their property, a relationship of trust was needed in which people are willing to concede their own power of individual coercion to a state which will maintain order on the basis of consent. This concept of government by trust and consent is, I think, one of the great contributions that Locke made to the development of political thought in the seventeenth and eighteenth centuries.

The other important thing that came in part out of the British tradition was what one might call the voluntary acceptance of obligation. Today it is fashionable to talk as if it was a new idea that rights have parallel obligations. It is not a new idea, although our present Government, quite rightly, espouses it. The idea of obligation, which is deeply embedded in the Christian and Jewish traditions, emerges very clearly in the history of political thought out of the work of Locke and his successors. One of the most amazing manifestations of this is the specifically English tradition of the constable, with every citizen having the power of arrest. Even today, the concept of a citizen's arrest is alive and thriving in our idea of law. It is very unusual – it is not a feature of most other countries – and is part of the idea that the citizen is responsible for maintaining law and order in his own society himself, rather than passing it over to the forces of the State to be coercive and to oblige people to obey the structure of order.

In all the developments I have outlined so far, however – the idea of the rule of law, the idea of participative citizens, the idea of the rights of the citizen, the idea of the obligations of the citizen – there was something very important missing, and that something has only been addressed in the twentieth century.

Let us go back, for a moment, to the Greeks. The Greeks, in particular under the emperor Caracalla, saw citizenship as something that depended upon a person being of a certain age, of a certain standing in the community, certainly male and certainly Greek, and therefore it was a very confined concept of citizenship. Democracy, yes, for probably about one-eighth of the adult residents of the Athenian Republic. The other seven-eighths were women, slaves or domestic servants and, as such, could not be considered 'citizens'. The Roman Empire was more generous, but even there only a section of society were citizens and specifically, of course, women and domestic servants (including male domestic servants) were not so regarded.

Even after the French Revolution there were clear limitations. A distinguished actress called Olympe de Gouges proposed a Declaration of the Rights of Women and Citizenesses in 1791, two years after the French Revolution. It was laughed out of court by the constituent assembly. Imagine that a woman might be a citizen in revolutionary France! Such are the limitations of even the most revolutionary mind, and it has taken our own twentieth century, with all its sins and its virtues, to perceive that citizenship is part of what it means to be a fully responsible adult human being, regardless of one's gender, race, origin, property or education. If you look back at the twentieth century, one of the absolutely staggering facts about it is that universal adult franchise was only achieved as late as the period around the First World War, and then only in a few countries. It says a great deal about the limitations of our concept of citizenship that this should be so.

Let us look now at the current position of the modern citizen. One of the characteristics of modern citizenship is that it comes at many levels. In the twenty-first century, being the citizen just of a nation state is not going to be an adequate expression of that concept for two reasons: partly because, as the nation state comes under huge pressure to devolve power downwards and also to concede power upwards (in the British case, to devolve downwards to the regions and to devolve upwards towards the European Union), citizens will possess rights protected by laws under different jurisdictions, and will incur obligations similarly. Each citizen, in addition to the duties required by international and national laws, owes a debt of obligation to his or her own community.

When you look back at the wonderful physical manifestations of municipal pride (go and look at any nineteenth-century town hall anywhere in the British Isles and you will see what I mean) – the proud, confident faces of the municipal leaders, the plaques, the memorials on graves, the sense of what it is to be a citizen of Liverpool, Manchester, Stafford or London, that pride which was such a crucial part of a confident democracy in the nineteenth century has been horribly eroded in our own. Today local government is much constrained. It is perceived often to be corrupt, it is perceived often to be subject to government guidelines, and that is true of governments of both parties. Pride in local government, however, is the first building-block of citizenship.

The second building-block of citizenship is the citizenship of one's region or country. In the United Kingdom that is much more meaningful in Scotland (which, of course, is a country as well as a region), or in Wales, or, in a rather less defined way, in the southwest or northeast of England than it is in many other parts of the country. The southeast of England has a tendency to lack regional spirit; it still remains essentially a satellite around London. But make no mistake: at least in my view, regional identity is going to become stronger and stronger, not least because increasingly regions are linking up directly to Brussels and no longer wishing to go through London. It has been a major factor in Scotland's wish to be in charge of itself, a devolved parliament in a devolved United Kingdom.

Let me say one more thing about the citizen of the community and the citizen of the region. (Of course, the concept of a region has developed further in France and Spain than it has in the United Kingdom, and in Germany it takes the form of federal structures – the German Länder or provinces.) It is a terribly important point. In our extraordinarily rapidly moving modern world, there is an intense desire to belong. The philosopher Ralph Dahrendorf, who is a colleague of mine in the House of Lords, put it beautifully in his book called *Life Chances*. He said that two things define the way people live if they have a satisfactory life: one is opportunities (in the modern world people long for opportunity, to better themselves, to choose, to advance, to experience new things), but the other thing, which people neglect, is what he called 'links'. The links with your family, your city, your district, your party, your church, your beliefs, stabilize a world that is energized by opportunity. If you have opportunity without links, you have a neurotic, restless and selfish society. But links without opportunity produce stagnation. A balance is what you need in order to make a good society. The need to belong is something that we have to try to understand.

I must say something about the impact of globalization on citizenship. The key political fact about globalization is that the political leaders of sovereign states no longer have power to implement many of the decisions that come before them. We pretend to ourselves that they do; they pretend to themselves that they do. They do not. They are like so many Canutes shouting at the rising tide. Time after time the decisions that confront us will be decided by the international financial markets, by speculators (as happened when John Major tried to enter the European Exchange Rate Mechanism), by co-operation between nation states (as in the Iraq crisis) which can begin to run itself in an almost self-perpetuating way.

Globalization therefore presents us with a huge and difficult question: How do we begin to construct the concept of the global citizen, the global rule of law, the global order? Do we do it by consent or are we driven to doing it only by coercion, by the re-creation of another great power, or concert of great powers, that can instruct us how to live?

Global citizenship is a very weak concept. For example, in Bosnia today many war criminals walk free. Time and again Mr Justice Golding, that distinguished South African judge, begged the international community to bring these men and women to justice, to bring them before an international trial. The international community, by which we mean the United States, Europe, Japan and a few others, do not listen, do not want to hear, because they do not know what they can do with a global order based on the rule of law, and they are scared about its implications.

I will say this (and it may be the most important point I make): if we cannot begin to construct an international rule of law, be it about war criminals in Bosnia, about banning genocide, about stopping land mines, or about effectively dealing with the environmental challenge, if we do not create the idea of global citizenship to match a global economy, there will not be a twenty-second century at all.

I want to end by saying something about education for citizenship – a few words about the UK, and a few words about the other levels of citizenship out there, which we do not really address much at all.

In the UK there has always been a problem about the education of citizens, and that is because we do not have an easy, finite subject to teach. If I go to an American school (and I went to one for three years as a child), I know that every single school day begins with the children standing up and saying, 'I believe in one country, indivisible, under God, with liberty and justice for all.' It is parroted, but they all know very broadly about the American Constitution, which is a specific document.

In South Africa three years ago, I was overwhelmingly impressed to see tiny little leaflets, no bigger than my hand, poured out in their millions, containing the basic bones of the South African Constitution – the new post-apartheid Constitution. The equivalent of our sixth-form pupils were running around the towns, villages, townships and communities of South Africa, carrying hundreds of these tiny Constitutions and offering them to every single person who wanted one. The result has been that South Africa, a country where half its people are illiterate, is – to put it bluntly – better educated in citizenship than the people of the United Kingdom, because the Government of Nelson Mandela went out of its way to ensure that every South African citizen knew, in some basic way, what his or her rights and obligations were.

When I was Secretary of State for Education, I tried to get going something called 'Education in Politics'. We got the HMIs (school inspectors) to develop it; we helped to create something called the Politics Society; we brought teachers into it; we conducted teacher-training seminars for them – and the initiative did not survive my departure because it was condemned as bringing party politics into schools. It was not seen as education for citizenship, which is what I had intended, but as a crude form of party propaganda. Sadly, through the old, endless adversarialism of the British system, something that was desperately needed was destroyed because the parties perceived it as being to the advantage of one or the other.

For 10 years the new national curriculum had no element of citizenship education in it whatsoever. It was only with Curriculum Paper No. 8 that the first reference was made to citizenship as one element in the broad, general studies of the curriculum – still hedged in all the time by the pressure of exams, the pressure of school league tables, the pressures on teachers to devote all their time to getting their youngsters through A levels, GCSEs and so on. Bluntly, this is ludicrous. We have created a mechanistic system of education which does not allow anything like enough room for the things that matter most to our children – i.e. some understanding of citizenship, some understanding of the moral universe, some understanding of the world in which they live. This is not just addressed to the previous Government. It is addressed much more generally to what has become an excessively quantitative way of measuring what education is all about.

Let me say a word about European citizenship, another area where I feel somewhat scarred by my own experience. In 1984 I brought together a group of teachers from the different member-states – 12 of them – of what was then the European Community. Britain had joined 12 years before. We brought those teachers together (and they were some of the best teachers that any country could provide) in a voluntary curriculum study group of about 40 people. We hammered out a European ecology course on video which summed up the ecology and geography of this new Europe. It was a beautiful video. Some of the best teachers in the whole of the continent had put their minds together to create it. It ranged from the city states of Italy to the great stretches of the Baltic Sea, and it had within it some of the things that make Europe a continent with an extraordinarily rich history. It was linked up to the BBC's technological innovation of the time, the so-called Doomsday Project, and an interactive version of the video was produced. One of the most exciting things about this was that a child could see the video in any one of eight languages simply by pushing a button. So it was a wonderful teaching machine, as well, for the languages of Europe.

I do not say this with any great bitterness, given her philosophy, but the project was vetoed by Mrs Thatcher. She said, in effect, that education was no part of the Community's responsibilities and that she would not allow this project to go ahead. I went to see Monsieur Delors, then the President of the Commission. I pleaded with him and he responded that he had too many battles with Madame Thatcher; he could not fight another one. So there has never been, from that day to this, any form of education for our children in what it is to be part of the

European Union. This is nothing to do with whether you like it or dislike it, with whether you want EMU or not – but it is difficult to have a referendum of our citizens concerning an issue about which they know virtually nothing. The last Government refused to allow any information campaign about EMU to be brought into this country.

I would like to conclude with a word on world citizenship. It is a terribly flawed instrument, but it is the only one we have and it is called the United Nations. We have nothing else. All of us can point the finger at it. All of us can complain about it. All of us look to it when there is some international crisis and we sit there and say, 'What's the Secretary General going to do about it? What's the Security Council going to do about it? What are we going to do to stop war coming to the Middle East?' Yet we do not teach our children much about the UN; the Council for Education of World Citizenship (the major vehicle for teaching people about the UN) is starved of even the tiniest, peanut-sized fund – it gets virtually nothing from any public source.

Despite this, as I have tried to explain, we are, like all other developed and developing countries, being pulled faster than we understand into a globalized economic world in which the nation state will essentially be overwhelmed – not necessarily swept away, but overwhelmed in the same way that a rock is overwhelmed by the rising tide. We have no idea how to create the political framework to deal with this, no idea about how to save democracy, which is founded on the concept of the nation state, and we do not have a great deal of time to get it right, to put those political and democratic frameworks in place. I have a very strong sense that the time is later than most of us think. It is certainly about time that we trusted our children to be educated as citizens in a way that virtually none of us had the privilege or the opportunity to be.

CITIZENSHIP FOR A NEW GENERATION

Martyn Lewis

18 MARCH 1998

Martyn Lewis CBE is a journalist and broadcaster who has presented all the mainstream news bulletins on ITV and BBC. A former chairman of Drive For Youth, he founded Youthnet UK, whose internet site 'The Site' offers information to young people seeking any kind of opportunity and help.

Citizenship is a subject which has to be a high priority for any civilized society, but all too often it languishes on the back burner in a world of competing political priorities. That is surprising when you consider that citizenship and politics share one great ideal, summed up best by Sir Winston Churchill's splendid rhetorical question, 'What is the use in living unless you can leave the world a better place for those who come after?' It took another politician to encapsulate the difficulty of that grand task. Edmund Burke pointed out that 'those who carry out great public works must be proof against the most fatiguing delays, the most shocking insults, the most mortifying disappointments, but, above all, the presumptuous judgement of the ignorant upon their designs'.

Up until now, citizenship has not been seriously entrenched in the political agenda, and it has no regular home on the national journalistic agenda either. Those two inadequacies conspire to leave the momentum for understanding citizenship pootling along in the slow lane of life, while public attention is diverted by a kaleidoscope of day-to-day problems hurtling past in the fast lane. In a busy world, mainstream news tends to be dominated by those problems, with all too little attention paid to news-worthy potential solutions, many of which would have strong elements of the concept of citizenship at their heart (although I must say that I do detect, in some quarters, an encouraging shift in the right direction).

All politicians want all of us to be good citizens, and yet collectively, over the years, they have put minimal effort into ingraining in us – at all levels – a total concept of the responsibil-ities that are the hallmark of good citizenship. Sticking plasters are stuck over problems; learned committees are set up, special charities and foundations are formed, all probing and examining the question from every angle, commissioning reports, coming up with a welter of splendid ideas and recommendations. Yet we still do not have a total package implemented at national level, planned and scrupulously carried out over a decade or more (because that is what is needed), in order to effect a permanent change in attitude which would bring all of us together as a nation to achieve basic levels of personal behaviour and commu-nity co-operation.

It is happening in pockets – in the town of Poyntzpass in Northern Ireland, for example, where Catholics and Protestants have lived and worked together in an exemplary way, and which you probably first heard of only because of the recent murder of two men whose long-standing friendship bridged the sectarian divide. It is happening in great charitable endeavours, where small armies of volunteers dedicate themselves to a wide variety of causes, helping their communities in all kinds of different ways. But there seems to be an unspoken view from the top that virtue will spread of its own accord, that good examples of citi-zenship will inspire others, and that there is no need to give the concept of citizenship the permanent national platform it needs to thrust it into every sector of the community – particularly towards those whose background and instincts encourage them to destroy instead of to build and help.

The world of good citizenship must be open to everyone, and must make a particular effort to reach out and embrace the most disaffected and disadvantaged. They are not just unemployed, they are right at the very bottom of the unemployment barrel – ill-educated youngsters already on the edge of crime and drugs. They are, by definition, the most difficult to reach, recruit and change into useful members of society, but, if we do not take the time – and expense – to turn them around, we are actively breeding and encouraging the criminals and vandals of tomorrow; we are doing nothing less than bequeathing to one generation after another a permanent legacy of damage and destruction. Governments have tended to put these young people on the back burner precisely because they are the most difficult and expensive to reach. It is a natural political instinct to want to reduce unemployment, and usually financial priorities dictate that this should be done as cheaply and quickly as possible. Systems and incentives are therefore set up which cream young people off the top of the unemployment pile, and leave many of those at the bottom untouched by the lifeboats of help, thus storing up much more damage to the fabric of society in years to come.

I speak with some passion and experience about this because, for 11 years, I was closely involved with Drive For Youth, one of a small group of charities specializing in this area of deep disadvantage. I want to tell you a little about the work carried out by dedicated and talented teams of trainers, because it shows that even the most desperate cases can be turned into good citizens keen to help others in their community – the kicks they got from being aimless and destructive replaced by the buzz and excitement of making constructive contributions to help others whose needs, in different ways, are just as great as theirs once were.

Drive For Youth was in the business of turning around young people between the ages of 18 and 26 who have been out of work for at least a year, and often two, three or even five years.

Many come from difficult backgrounds and are caught in a whirlpool of deprivation and despair. Most are on the fringes of crime and drugs. They have no concept of citizenship because they have no concept of belonging to any part of society. Over and over again we identify one strong characteristic: a sullen selfishness, perhaps the last protective fence they have erected around the inadequacies they believe they have. School has done nothing for them. More often than not, their families – if they have one – have not helped, or have not been able to help, by providing the core of support most of us need while growing up. They are bitter and deeply disillusioned.

Nonetheless, after the Drive For Youth experience, over 60 per cent of them go into jobs or further education – and, if you include as an outcome going back to do regular voluntary work in their community, that figure rises to over 90 per cent. What makes most of them come out at the other end of a 17-week course ready to play their part in society as responsible citizens? These are the ingredients:

- Outdoor pursuits where the emphasis is on working as a team, thinking about others – possibly for the first time in their lives – and appreciating their differences and strengths, and working for each other, not just themselves.
- Personal counselling to show them – again, probably for the first time in their lives – that someone with a real ability and determination to help really cares about them.
- Careers advisers who ride shotgun to them throughout the course, so they can give better advice about their final direction and help them into the next stage on the road to a job.
- Experienced personnel staff from local companies who give them all the advice they need about interview techniques and CVs (many of the youngsters have never even heard about CVs).
- Finally, and probably the most important catalyst of all, work on community projects in different parts of Britain, such as

building forestry footpaths for the disabled, or clearing the ground for a new hospice – meeting and helping, in a wide variety of ways, people who, through illness or disability, appear visibly worse off than they are, but who have developed a much more positive attitude towards life. It is usually the first time these youngsters have met such people at close quarters, and it has a profound effect on them.

The lesson is that these young people, representing a 'worst-case scenario', become better citizens – more tolerant, more understanding, more confident, more ambitious – by becoming more aware, in practical terms, of what potential lies beyond the narrow confines of the intensely negative and difficult corner of the world in which they grew up. To be a good citizen you need to know how and where you might fit into the jigsaw, the framework, of your country, and that your country values the contribution you make.

This does not just apply to the deeply disadvantaged young people whom Drive For Youth helped. It applies to young people everywhere who, in taking the vital decisions that will shape the kind of adult they become and the kind of career they follow, need clear, comprehensive, easily accessible information about the full range of opportunities and help available in Britain today. The chances of making the most of their lives are maximized if they can tap into such an information source. Such a database does exist now. It grew out of the needs identified at Drive For Youth, but now spreads far beyond those to encompass every area of youth activity, ambition and need. It is a charity in its own right – called YouthNet UK – and it is so new that many are still unaware of its existence.

If you are a young person today seeking any form of opportunity for help, who do you turn to for advice? You turn to your parents and other relatives, their friends, your teachers, or perhaps youth workers. But, by definition, their knowledge is limited. They might direct you to two or three organizations that can help; they will not be able to tell you that there are perhaps 20 or 30 such organizations you should be contacting and exploring. Limited knowledge means limited choices. Yet surely you make better key decisions about your future – decisions which, after all, shape your life, your career and the kind of person you become – if you are presented with the full range of options for pursuing your particular interest. YouthNet is designed to fill that gap, to make those choices less of a hit-and-miss affair.

We have created a special site on the internet. It is not called 'YouthNet', because detailed research about young people's likes and preferences tells us that they cannot stand the word 'youth' – it smacks of a label pinned on them by adults and many find it hugely patronizing. We looked around and, to our amazement, found that even with 40 million people using the internet world-wide, no one had registered the name 'The Site'. So we grabbed it ourselves, and registered it worldwide. With the help of £133,000 of National Lottery money and a great deal of corporate support, we set about designing our dream site, cherry-picking the very best software and equipment from computer companies that are deadly rivals (IBM, Microsoft, Netscape, Sun, Oracle) and persuading them to give it to us free of charge – half a million pounds worth in all. Incidentally, no one over the age of 23 worked on the actual design for our website, so it has been created by young people for young people. That design places huge emphasis on ease and speed of access, and this is also helped by the fact that our server is maintained by Imperial College London's computer department and is placed on the very spine of the internet – a privilege normally granted only to universities and government departments.

Accessing the information you want on The Site could not be simpler. Because we have incorporated in our software the electronic postcoding of Britain, you simply tap in your post-code, the area in which you are seeking opportunity or help, the distance you are prepared to travel to pursue that, other optional details such as wheelchair access – and within seconds you are presented with a list of options, brief descriptions of the organizations that can help, plus details of how they can help and how you can get in touch. Within the next few months we shall be incorporating in our software the Ordnance Survey mapping – and street-mapping – of the whole of Britain. You will be able to print out a map saying, 'You are here, and the organization you want to find is here.' In addition, if those organizations have their own websites offering even greater details, you can automatically move across to them just by clicking on their names. Our system removes the need to know the often complicated website addresses of organizations offering the assistance you want.

The Site has one over-riding principle: we do not believe in reinventing the wheel. Much of our data comes from information partners, experts in their field who already maintain their own databases, such as Resource Information Services, the Help For Health Trust, the Sports Councils of England, Scotland and Wales. We have set up special links with them so that their computers can talk to ours at least once a week. Smaller community organizations, such as those on the Isle of Dogs, which were planning to set up their own computer systems listing the full range of community services available in their area, have instead simply asked us to put that information on The Site – at a fraction of the cost. We have a promising pilot project under way assessing the potential for us to include all the information stored by Citizen's Advice Bureaux right across the country, with all their offices linked directly to The Site.

We are also talking to Neighbourhood Watch at a national level; to the new Drugs Unit recently set up by the Government; to the Home Office and the Department of Education and Employment, about linking everyone in the country who wants to volunteer with the appropriate nearest volunteering opportunity; and we have been chosen as the main means for disseminating basic information on the New Deal for the young unemployed, with that information updated daily. We are closely involved in plans by Newcastle and Birmingham City Councils to set up a network of interactive information booths, linked to key sites on the internet, right across their cities.

The Site is proving to be of help in other ways too. A company approached us to say that it wanted to offer support to a charity helping people with learning difficulties within a 10-kilometre radius of its office. Could we tell them what was out there that fitted the bill? Within minutes we had identified and faxed to them details and contact points for no fewer than seven such opportunities.

We have over 14,000 organizations on our database so far. That will double within the next few months, and by the millennium we expect to include details of well over 100,000 organizations stretching right down to community level in every part of the United Kingdom. Already, with virtually no publicity – because we have only just reached what we considered a critical mass of helpful information – we are getting 20,000 hits a day on our website.

There it is: a clear, definitive database, maximizing the choices for character- and career-forming decisions, making people more aware of what they can do to help themselves and others, giving them instant access to the full range of options, enhancing their potential to be better citizens. The Site is delivering a unique service. There is nothing else remotely like it anywhere else in the world, and other countries – among them Ireland, the United States and the European Commission – are exploring its potential for themselves. We believe The Site will be a powerful force for encouraging people to be better citizens, by opening up a wide range of opportunities of which they might not normally be aware.

How, though, do young people themselves view the whole issue of citizenship? My answer here is anecdotal, and relies on a more personal kind of experience as the father of two teenage girls. The elder is now 22, but I remember well a particular conversation I had with her when she started her gap year before university. She has, incidentally, had the benefit of a good education; she has a lively, enquiring mind (laced with regular, and wholly commendable, streaks of stubbornness); she talks to her mother and father about everything (at least we think she does!); she does not smoke, and has resisted the repetitive offers of soft drugs that, according to a recent report, touch the lives of 70 per cent of our schoolchildren; she is a thoughtful person who cares about others and their problems. I would like to think she is growing up to be a good citizen. Indeed, she went on to spend the first half of her gap year doing emotionally difficult and character-forming work as a volunteer at Great Ormond Street Children's Hospital.

Before she started that work, I asked her what the word 'citizenship' – the business of being a good citizen – meant to her and her friends.

Her reply was this: 'It doesn't mean anything. We don't even think about it.'

I pressed her further. 'Well,' she said, 'I suppose you become a citizen when you start paying taxes.'

We talked on:

Question: 'At any stage in your schooling, were you taught what would make you a good citizen – what your rights and responsibilities in society might be?'

Answer: 'Well, in primary school we were taught to be polite, how to address people, to give up our seats on the bus to older people – things like that. But in secondary school – nothing! We never discussed rights and responsibilities and citizenship except perhaps in the very occasional debate.'

Question: 'What about respect for your country's institutions?'

Answer: 'Young people today don't respect institutions just because they're institutions. It's not as automatic as it might have been in your day. They have to earn respect; they have to be seen to be doing things that are for the good of society. There's no point in having tradition just for the sake of it. Every institution that asks for respect and affection and loyalty has to earn that – and keep on earning it.'

Question: 'What is the most important thing that could be done to make you and your friends feel a sense of citizenship – of being part of your country and contributing to it?'

Answer (and this surprised me): 'A sense of citizenship would be brought across more clearly if there was some kind of service that had us focusing on our country – on its needs and traditions. My French, Italian and Spanish friends tell me about the year they have to spend giving service of some kind to their country, if not military, then some kind of social service. It seems to be compulsory, at least for men, unless they go to study abroad.'

Question: 'But would you and your friends like it if something like that was compulsory?'

Answer: 'Maybe, maybe not – but we would do it if we had to. And if it was the right kind of service, we would understand more about Britain, more about ourselves too, and perhaps at the end of it that new understanding would make us feel as proud about our country as our European friends seem to be about theirs.'

Those answers are, of course, anecdotal rather than representing a carefully researched point of view. Yet the concept of a national requirement for a substantial period of 'service' to your country, either during a gap in studies or work, or even running parallel to them – without being too prescriptive as to what form it might take – would, I think, do much to create some seeds of citizenship in early life that would have a good chance of flourishing throughout adult life.

I have also seen at close quarters a third kind of young person – out of work since leaving school, disadvantaged, feeling excluded from society in the same way as our Drive For Youth youngsters, but angry too, very angry, and finding him- or herself in the company of many others who feel the same. Let me paint the picture.

A desperately deprived neighbourhood; a trigger point that sends anger spilling over the edge into mass violence. There are many places that come to mind, but I am talking about Los Angeles five years ago, one year to the day after the infamous riots. People of goodwill were trying to build something better from the ruins. Community leaders, politicians, businessmen and social workers were called to a two-hour problem-solving debate in a community hall at the heart of the riot area. The debate was carried live on K-Cal, Channel Nine, the local TV station. My wife and I had the privilege of observing the proceedings from two seats at the back.

It seemed to be going reasonably well. Proposals, ideas and explanations buzzed around the room. Then, one hour into the debate, a door at the back burst open. Security guards were brushed aside like flies, and in came seven youngsters, all built like Schwarzenegger, wearing sleeveless vests, with red bandannas round their foreheads. They were instantly recognizable to the local people as one of the most notorious gangs in the neighbourhood. An involuntary, collective intake of breath added to the tension. The Secret Service agents guarding the then Commerce Secretary Ron Brown, who had just flown in from Japan to take part in the debate, reached towards their shoulder holsters. But what followed was not violent – it was a cry from the heart, a cry which is increasingly being picked up by young people everywhere and which, I would suggest, offers another possible key to the door of good citizenship.

The television moderator broke the stunned silence with words that did not quite capture the mood of the occasion. 'Is there anything you gentlemen would like to say?'

Well, yes, there certainly was. The gang's leader said they had been watching the debate on television. They did not have much confidence in the politicians and their promises, because most of the politicians there had been largely responsible – as they saw it – for the policies that created the deprivation and sense of hopelessness in their neighbourhoods. He actually put it rather more strongly than that, and at greater length too. But he went on to make a remarkable offer on primetime television. He acknowledged that he and his gang had created big trouble in the past, but said they were now prepared to channel their energies into helping to build up their community instead of destroying it. 'Just give us young people a chance,' he said, and he used what has become something of a buzz word: 'empowerment'. 'Give us a role to play, constructive things to do within our communities, empower us – and we, the young people of Los Angeles, will not let you down.'

It was electrifying! It won huge applause from most of the audience. It transformed the debate. And afterwards, when the camera had been switched off, those in authority talked as never before to those whose main purpose in the past seemed to have been to attack authority.

Coincidentally, a week later the *New York Times* reported that gang leaders from all over the States – and this could only happen in America – had held a convention in Kansas City, at which they publicly pledged to do all they could to turn their negative activities into positive ones. Again the key word was 'empowerment' and, interestingly, the kicks they got from being destructive were clearly being replaced by the boost they got from being interviewed and reported in the media as would-be heroes with a job to do out there in the community. That gathering did not by any means include all the gang leaders, but it was a start.

Could we not explore here in Britain whether some of the gangs who haunt parts of our cities could be approached, to test the potential for them to take on environmental or other projects that would be a help to the community? Idealistic? Perhaps, but we will not know until we try. It is surely worth a shot on a trial basis.

Whether young people are members of gangs or not, I believe the main key to turning them, whatever their background, into good citizens is to involve them formally and regularly in service to the community. I am talking about real empowerment –

giving the right young people a higher responsibility, at an earlier age than some conventional wisdom acknowledges them to be ready for it. Let them do it in tandem with school work or jobs, and particularly make sure that they do it if they are unable to find a job. We need to look hard (and I know a great deal of work is already going on in this area) at ways in which we can more thoroughly match young people to the areas of community service that would be of most benefit to them and their country. We can help turn them into good citizens by enabling even those who do not have jobs to make a useful contribution to society, and thus feel they are a part of that society, actually involved in the very business of citizenship.

Amongst the many conclusions from a recent collection of splendid essays by the Institute for Citizenship Studies is this: an important part of countering alienation and contempt is to reconnect citizens and society. There are many references in the essays to the importance of active involvement in voluntary associations and societies. There is now a substantial body of research which draws attention to the importance of civil society – that network of voluntary organizations and interests which stands between us as individuals and the framework of the State. These organizations are what root us in wider society, and the evidence tells us that an active civil society (only part of which is ever directly concerned with politics) is key to building the trust which needs to exist between the governed and those who govern. Democracy represents a continuing relationship, and is something much deeper than the occasional visit to the ballot box.

That sums up the immediate challenge to us today, and especially to the current generation of young people. But what about generations to come? Is there anything further we can do to instil in them the fuller sense of citizenship that appears to be lacking in today's more troublesome teenagers?

For a start, I would find a bigger and better showcase for the many people in communities all over Britain who, year after year, visibly deliver fine examples of citizenship at the highest level. I would suggest a thorough trawl of other countries to hunt down good, practical examples of community involvement. In Norway, for example, all school parents get together once a year to spend an entire day painting the classrooms in the schools their children attend. The day finishes with a big barbecue in the playground, also provided by the parents. What a great idea! So why not think up a whole host of projects that cement this sense of community, of responsibilities shared – and save the government some expense as well?

In parts of Holland, some of the unemployed – in return for their social security payments – are sent out on neighbourhood watch patrols, helping to police the streets and making them safer for the entire community. It not only serves as a useful social function, it also cuts through the stigma of joblessness to make them feel they are contributing in an important and much appreciated way to the wellbeing of their community.

Much depends on the media being prepared to highlight those examples of attempted solutions and good practice. A growing number do, especially among the regional press. The *Liverpool Post and Echo* springs to mind as a powerful example of what balanced news reporting – highlighting the positives alongside the inevitable negatives – can achieve. There is, however, still an unhealthy tendency in some national media outlets to create and maintain inaccurate stereotypes of parts of our society. To read them, you would sometimes think that all young people are football hooligans, joy-riders, vandals, muggers or murderers. And you would be left in ignorance of the powerful, dedicated and often highly interesting work being carried out by volunteers to address a wide variety of needs within their communities – examples of which are there to be grabbed in the many award ceremonies for community involvement. A culture where negativity dominates does nothing to encourage the ethos of good citizenship, and this may well be a factor in the difficulty those promoting that ethos have had in getting their message across in any substantial and effective way over the years.

Journalists are not vultures perched in some comfortable eyrie on a craggy peak, regularly swooping down to feed on the carcasses among the teeming masses below. We are not removed in some lofty way from the society on which we report. We are an integral part of that society and, as such, we have a duty to showcase its many newsworthy successes, triumphs and achievements alongside its failures, disasters and tragedies. I am not suggesting – indeed, I have never suggested – that we stop reporting the negative. I am simply suggesting that coverage should strike a more reasonable balance between that which goes wrong and that which goes right.

Some editors stand accused of wanting the worst to be true because that, they believe, is a better story. This infects other journalists – newcomers who, often reluctantly, fall into line because they are made to believe that this is the only way to get on in the profession, or even to keep their current jobs. So the pressure from the top traps large areas of journalism in a whirlpool of negativity. I would suggest that such pressure, where it is an unthinking gut reaction, is also a product of lazy journalism. It is often the easiest thing in the world to report a negative story, because the pictures and copy virtually fall into your lap. It is a much more difficult journalistic challenge – and one which some journalists refuse to face – to take a positive story of equivalent importance to society and turn it into a piece of really interesting journalism which people want to watch, hear or read.

We should never forget that where there is disaster, there are people trying to recover from it; where there is suffering, there are people trying to help; where there is conflict, there are people trying to end it; where things go wrong, there are people trying to put them right, and people trying to make sure that they do not happen again; and where there are mistakes and misjudgements, there are lessons being learnt, paving the way for potential success and achievement. I have long believed that the effect we would have on society by getting the positive and the negative in better balance could create a climate where citizenship could take off and flourish – to the greater good of all our lives.

I also find it incredible that knowledge of everyone's rights – and, more importantly, obligations – as citizens is not locked into every school curriculum in the country. There should be regular weekly lessons in citizenship for every class in every age group, gradually instilling in them, as they rise from kindergarten to sixth form, the full meaning of citizenship. The indications are that Bernard Crick's long-awaited report on citizenship is going to recommend something along those lines. It cannot come a moment too soon. That other report I mentioned by the Institute of Citizenship Studies also pointed out how remarkable it is that 'we do so little to educate the young into the ways of citizenship and the workings of democracy. The national curriculum nods in the direction of citizenship but gives it scant attention ... the aim should be for citizenship and democracy to become part of everyday life for future generations.'

Would such regular classes on citizenship work? Could the collective enthusiasm of all involved be both created and maintained? Could everyone agree on the precise shape, purpose and content of such classes? The answer is 'yes' – with one caveat. You have to give it time to work, time which stretches well beyond the lifetime of one Parliament. You have to give it not just a year or two, but perhaps seven to ten years.

To explain why, I have an example from Columbus, Ohio, which was considered some 25 years ago to be one of the shabbiest, filthiest cities in the United States. A new mayor, Dana Reinhart, respected and supported by both main political parties, came into office determined to tackle the problem. He started weekly classes at all levels in the city's schools. The subject was the importance to everyone of having a clean city, free of graffiti and vandalism. It took 13 years – a whole generation of schoolchildren – for the message to soak properly through the whole community. That year, Columbus, Ohio won the award for the cleanest, tidiest city in the whole of the United States.

It can be done. Let's put good citizenship high on the agenda, on a proud pedestal. Let's make it a target to reach for, until the pursuit of it becomes as natural as breathing. As a means to achieve that, we might consider some form of politically accept-able, regular community service – run, of course, with the help of adults, but wherever possible by the young people themselves. Let's challenge them, let's trust them more – empower them to organize, innovate and come up with ideas as part of this programme. And let us as a country back that effort with a commitment to establish a long-term educational framework in which citizenship is firmly related to everyday life and becomes substantially more than a worthy word to which people occa-sionally pay lip service. We should make sure that citizenship becomes an integral part of growing up – so that, in 13 years time, when anyone asks a class of 18-year-olds like my daughter what citizenship means to them, they are overwhelmed by the chorus of enthusiastic replies.

A GOVERNING VIEW

Frank Field

3 APRIL 1998

The Rt Hon. Frank Field is the Labour Member of Parliament for Birkenhead. Formerly the Minister for Welfare Reform (Labour 1997–8), he resigned his post to fight welfare reform issues from the back benches.

I wish to cover four main themes, all of which are contained within the framework of the Government's Green Paper on Welfare Reform. I want to talk first of all about what is negotiable and what is not negotiable and then about the approach to political activity that this Green Paper describes. Thirdly, I wish to touch on the theme of the Green Paper, which is about a new contract. Lastly – and this is implicit in the whole of the Green Paper – I want to discuss certain ideas about citizenship.

The Green Paper makes very clear what areas are not negotiable and what areas are negotiable by way of discussion, lobbying, listening and talking which will follow its publication. The first no-go area for the Government is that it is not prepared to negotiate its commitment to the poor. That is a clear theme which runs throughout the document and will do so throughout our stewardship. The second no-go area is that we are not prepared to back down from reform.

Reform is necessary, as the following examples illustrate. If you look at those who were claiming benefits after the establishment of the Coalition Government's and the Attlee Government's reforms in 1948, two-thirds of these were pensioner households. Today over two-thirds of those claiming minimum income support are of working age. A service which was designed quite properly to channel additional help very largely, almost exclusively, to pensioners is not a service which is adequate in today's turbulent world when over two-thirds of those claiming the minimum benefit are in fact of working age. In this sense, therefore – and in this very city of Liverpool, where we have three times the national average of households claiming income support and over twice the national average of those claiming incapacity benefit – clearly the Government's approach to welfare is particularly relevant.

Where, however, the Government believes that everything is negotiable is in the area of how we meet our objectives, how the reform programme should be built up and how that reform programme will be presented to the House of Commons – and enacted by Commons and Lords alike. Here everything is negotiable. It is not that we will come with open and empty minds, but rather that we will be presenting a whole series of proposals for discussion.

Those proposals will look, for example, at major reform of pensions and the fundamental reform of the Child Support Agency. Given that previous attempts at reform in this area have not – if I put it politely – met with success, a little humility here is certainly due. Although we will have proposals to put forward, we are anxious for those proposals to be exposed to the greatest possible public debate, so that the next attempts to legislate in this area are more securely based than before. There will also be a fundamental document presented on the strategy for countering fraud. In addition, we have promised the reform of incapacity benefit, and we are looking seriously at the 'gateways', as they are called, to Disability Living Allowance. In all these areas and many more, we will be bringing forward proposals. We wish those proposals to be discussed fully, frankly, strongly and, we hope, in a sense of friendship and fellowship.

This leads me to my second theme: the nature of the political process in implementing this whole programme of welfare reform, a process that will take many parliaments to achieve fully, although that is in no way an excuse for doing nothing now. The Green Paper sets out the new approach to political activity. It contains what are regarded as the Government's eight key principles governing all we will be doing in welfare reform. To give just two examples, we believe in the old verity that those who can work should work, full stop. We also believe that those who are poorest should gain the greatest help when taxpayers are thinking about what support they should deliver. That does not mean all other groups are excluded, but it does provide a focus when we look at the large Social Security budget of a hundred billion pounds which taxpayers meet. Our one other overriding aim is to ensure that, where taxpayers help out, the greatest help will go to those whose needs are greatest.

So there are eight principles for discussion and we intend, as we roll out the programme of reform, that you will be looking at the extent to which each individual programme locks on to those eight principles. As a rule, individual programmes must be consistent within the framework that we have laid down.

To ensure that there is a proper public debate, the Green Paper has published 32 success measurements. If, for example, the Government believes that those who can should work when they are able to, then clearly one of our success measurements should be to gauge whether we are seeing more people in work than out of work. Of course, while these success measurements are expressed in general terms so that you and I can understand them, we will need to move to a second stage where we try to firm up in more technical language what those general objectives are, so that, as time goes on, we can be held properly to account for our stewardship. There is, therefore, a tripartite programme of principles, policies (which will come before you as Green Proposals) and success measurements (so that you can gauge whether we are delivering or not, and so that we can gauge whether we are being successful or not). This is all part of the nature of the new politics in which this Government believes, and which is in part being unfolded by these welfare reform proposals.

That brings me to the third of the themes I wish to touch upon: the thread which links together all the pages and all the ideas in the Green Paper. It is about a new contract, a contract which is quite simply based on duties. Gone is that other language of rights and responsibilities. In comes, very clearly, the idea that contracts are about duties. They are not one-sided duties, nor is it a one-sided contract. To return to one of those principles I mentioned earlier: if we believe it is a duty that those who can work should work if they are able to do so, then there is a similar duty on us as Government and us as taxpayers to ensure that we have all the resources of Government focused on an employment-finding service which makes that task easier.

Similarly, if, as we know, the greater the skills you have, the less chance there is that you will be unemployed and the greater the chance you will have to be employed, then that puts certain duties on the Government concerning the way our schools and colleges behave and perform. Hence the targets for them. It also imposes duties concerning the facilities we are beginning to build up for those who gained least from formal education in their younger years. It is, then, a contract based on duties, but these duties are put on both sides. The individual has a duty, and the Green Paper lists what we similarly believe must be the Government's duty to ensure that individuals have the opportunities to meet the duties placed upon them. Our welfare reform movement is, therefore, based on the concept of a contract.

This leads me directly to my fourth theme: ideas about citizenship and the extent to which the Green Paper – and its reforms, its stance, the direction for which the Government seeks your approval – is beginning to change the nature of citizenship in this country. In some ways it is amazing to me that the citizenship which we now share has lasted and remained as secure as it has done in this country. The nature of citizenship as we know it was, in fact, a very un-British one. It was, in a sense, developed from the radical ideas which were most seriously seen in France, although they did have some currency in this country. Citizenship in France – from the time of the Revolution – was imposed from the centre; a code was established about citizenship. In this country, on the other hand, citizenship has been acquired. Think of our society as a cart, progressing into the future. At certain moments in history, that cart has slowed down enough for certain other people to be welcomed on board. In this way, citizenship and the rights of citizenship were built up very slowly in this country. It began to be conceded on a large scale, and then on a mass scale, partly as a result of the franchise reform movement of the last century, but also because of the welfare reforms which were initiated in the last century.

Long before David Alton tried to tell the people of Liverpool that collective action could actually occur which was nothing to do with the Government or the State, people in this country believed that you could extend protection by building up Friendly and Mutual Societies, which offered protection to whole groups of people, groups of members. Thanks to this movement, and this huge belief of the citizens that through self-help you could gain self-improvement, those who were most adamant against franchise reform began to lose their will to argue their point. They also saw that in the self-help and self-improvement movement there were already little democracies, self-governing organizations of citizens responsibly carrying out their tasks.

The whole ethos of the mutual aid movement was therefore one of the great reasons for the extraordinary push forward in the last decade of the nineteenth century and into the twentieth century. Those who had opposed the widening of the franchise had to admit that these groups had already won citizenship by what they had done. Thus, unlike in other countries where the franchise was imposed from the centre as a result of revolutionary movements, in this country it was built up from practical action whereby people showed that they were *worthy* of citizenship, to be confirmed *formally* by the franchise. Clearly they were already citizens, except in that respect. This has helped to form a citizenship which has been universal, and which has, I would contend, drifted on happily through most of the twentieth century.

It is now frayed at the edges, however, and there is a growing apprehension in this country that, if you award citizenship on this basis – i.e. everybody must be equal in whatever they do – then some people, maybe large numbers of people, may abuse that status which you are willingly affording to them and for which you are often paying. For this reason, I see the theme underlining the Green Paper, the theme that touches on citizenship (linked as it is to the idea of contract), as crucial to the survival of universal citizenship in this country.

Some may argue that the idea of contract contained in the Green Paper is all very well if you have the means to participate fully – but what about those who do not? I think that what we will see, as a result of the proposed contract for citizenship, is that we will in fact have two forms of citizenship in this country: a slightly shaky one as it is now, i.e. universal citizenship for everyone, and then, growing alongside that, the contract form of citizenship which is clearly embarked on in the Green Paper. Two things will happen, I hope.

One is that, as the contract takes root, the idea of citizenship will be reinforced, strengthened. In some areas where people felt that, perhaps, there should be disengagement, there will instead be a renewal of enthusiasm and support. People will also be asking, because of that first idea of citizenship, what will happen to those who cannot participate fully in the contract welfare outlined in the Green Paper. Therefore one of the tests will be the extent to which these reforms are *inclusive* and the extent to which they are *divisive*. I believe they will be inclusive, and I have an example to illustrate this.

This Government is utterly serious that those who can work should work. In London, for example, all along the tube line we had a 40 per cent unemployment rate amongst young people. The tubes carry advertisments for station assistants, aged 18 and over, beginning at a salary of £15,700. Now, either the labour market does not work – people do not travel on the tube like I do and see these advertisments, and the information is not getting where it should – or some people believe that they are beyond starting at £15,700 and that the task of station assistant is too lowly for them. That is not going to be an option under this Government. We believe that those who can work should take up work opportunities – with all the duties this also places on the Government to ensure that people can be effective in those opportunities.

While I have defined work up to now in terms of financial reward, we also know that there is a huge amount of work which is done but which is not paid – and this is called caring. Indeed, there would be no welfare worth talking of if people, in fellowship, in love, did not look after one another. There is no way that we, collectively as a community, can pay for that care. What we can do, however, if we have the will and the resolve, is to ensure that those who are caring do not, as a result of that act of altruism, take the low incomes they have as carers into desperate poverty in retirement. So, when the Green Paper on pensions is outlined, you will see that we extend what we mean as a Government, and what we hope you approve of as a community, when we talk of work. We wish to celebrate and reward those who are undertaking the most vital of all tasks in our community, i.e. caring for others. Under contract welfare, the citizenship of this group will be secured in the rights and contributions which we establish for carers. Specifically, as a community we will be ensuring that in the future carers will gain more adequate pensions.

Let me try to draw these themes together. As a Government we are not negotiating on our commitment to the poor – although clearly, in changed circumstances, the way we respond to that primary impulse will be different in some important respects from the last great reforming Liberal Government or the last great reforming Labour Government. The *processes* of reform are, however, negotiable. We hope to strengthen our loyal backbenchers in Parliament and learn from the voting public in this whole process, both to breathe greater life into democracy and also to make a better reform programme. The nature of politics is changing. The Government is clearly setting out its principles of welfare reform and laying out how it should try to measure success. In acting so, it will improve the Government's performance while at the same time allowing it to be directly accountable to voters as the next election approaches.

I hope I have communicated something of how central this new contract is to the welfare reform process. I also wish to make clear that it is not confined to the topic of welfare reform, but is part of the emerging debate about how citizenship can be renewed and secured in this country. The Government believes that the form of citizenship which we have inherited – which has largely been taken for granted and which is universally bestowed, with little said after it has been given to people – is one which by itself cannot safely see us into the new century. It needs to be buttressed, to be strengthened by the idea of contract citizenship. In pursuing this approach, the aim of the Government is to engage with the public. It entails turning our backs on the hardening of hearts we have witnessed for a couple of decades. Our goals centre around the universality of citizenship, which was formally endorsed as part of our political culture with the franchise reforms. Our aim is to value that idea of a universal citizenship securely into the next century.

THE HEBREW TRADITION

Jonathan Sacks

22 APRIL 1998

Dr Jonathan Sacks is the Chief Rabbi of the British Commonwealth. He is the author of Faith in the Future[1] *and* The Politics of Hope[2].

Let me begin, as is our Jewish custom, on a slightly lighter note. This is my favourite story of all time, a story I heard first when I was an undergraduate studying philosophy.

There was a wonderful man, Professor David Daube, who was at that time Regius Professor of Roman Law at Oxford. He said to me, 'What are you studying, Sacks?'

I replied, 'Philosophy.'

'Oh, dear dear,' he said. 'Philosophers never know what day of the week it is, their head in the clouds. I will tell you a story. Who is your hero?'

'Wittgenstein,' I said, being a Cambridge philosopher in the 1960s.

'Oh,' he said. 'It happened one day that Wittgenstein and two of his disciples, Professor Hart and Professor Elizabeth Anscombe, were standing on Oxford station waiting for the London train. They were so engrossed in their metaphysical speculation that they entirely failed to notice the train as it steamed into the

---

[1] J. Sacks, *Faith in the Future* (London: Darton, Longman & Todd, 1995).
[2] J. Sacks, *The Politics of Hope* (London: Jonathan Cape, 1997).

platform, failed to notice as it stood there, and only as it began to steam out did they look up to see the train.

'Professor Hart ran and caught the train. Elizabeth Anscombe, an enormous woman, ran and caught the train. Wittgenstein ran and ran, but could not catch the train up. He stood there on the platform, forlorn and looking utterly devastated.

'A lady, seeking to comfort him, came up to him and said, "Don't worry, there'll be another train in an hour's time."

'Wittgenstein replied, "But you don't understand: they came to see *me* off." '

I inferred from this that it is sometimes good to stand back and ask ourselves where we are going and why. I want to do some very simple things here, to discuss the concept of a free society, to discuss a distinction I made in my most recent book between a social contract and a social covenant, and to touch on the associated idea of responsibilities as against rights. I want to do this from a specifically religious perspective – indeed, from a Jewish perspective. Let me explain why.

Two traditions have shaped the civilization of the West. The first is ancient Greece, the second is ancient Israel. When we come to politics, we are familiar with the enormous contribution of the Greek thinkers, above all Plato and Aristotle. The word 'politics' itself, like the word 'citizen', like the word 'democracy', betrays its Hellenistic roots – all these words come from Greek and Latin. Our political philosophy, our habit of thinking, is heavily Hellenistic.

There is a second tradition, however, the Jewish tradition, which in some respects is no less important but is far less well understood. I want to say that it is worth studying it, at least for a few moments, because of three things. The first is that, whereas Greek thought and indeed Western thought has been preoccupied with a single concept above all others, namely the State, Jewish thought has been more interested in the concept of society – or perhaps, as we might say now, the community. I find it very interesting, for instance, that the greatest of Greek thinkers,

Aristotle, famously said that man is a 'political animal', whereas the most famous of Jewish thinkers, Moses Maimonides, said that man is a 'social animal'. What is the difference between State and society? That is one thing I want to talk about.

The second thing is that Greek thought is particularly interested in power. Both Plato and Aristotle define citizenship in terms of ruling and being ruled. Judaism, by contrast, is much more interested in the limits of power, specifically the moral limits, the limits set by the idea that ultimately the final sovereign authority is God himself. That is going to lead me into distinguishing between a contract between the State and its citizens, and a covenant between God and people, in which all citizens are equal in the Republic of the Good.

The third thing is that, whereas the Greeks had philosophers, of course Ancient Israel had prophets. The prophets differ from the philosophers in one significant respect: the philosophers tend to talk about timeless truths (never invite a philosopher for dinner – they will always be late), while the prophets always see truths as realized in time and history. In fact, prophets are the first people – and still the most powerful – who saw history itself as a story, a narrative, a journey towards redemption. And they, much more than the philosophers, understood how often we get deflected from that journey.

I want to begin, therefore, with a word about the journey itself, and it is an odd point. In the Jewish calendar at the moment, we stand not only on the brink of Holocaust Day, but also in the middle of a very interesting period of time which is called in the Bible 'the counting of the Omer' – the 49 days between Passover and the festival we call Pentecost. Interestingly, the Bible tells us that we have to *count* the days between these two festivals. This is the verse, and it does not exactly sound political: 'From the day after the Sabbath, the day after the festival, the day we brought the sheaf of the wave offering, you shall count seven complete weeks, count fifty days till the day after the seventh week, and then present an offering of new grain to the Lord.'

What is significant about that sentence? The significance is that in ancient Israel the calendar was linked not just to the seasons, but also to historical events and, indeed, to a journey of the Israelites – not only through time, but also through a stage of moral maturity. According to this mode of understanding, the seven weeks between Passover and Pentecost are very significant. Passover is the festival in which we commemorate the Exodus from Egypt. Pentecost is when we commemorate the giving of the divine law at Mount Sinai. By saying that we have to connect those two events by counting the days between them, the Bible is telling us that they are not two separate events, but part of a single journey.

On Passover, the Israelites achieved freedom in a very specific sense – they were released from slavery, they were liberated from tyranny. Still to this day we remember and re-enact that moment by eating the unleavened bread of affliction and the bitter herbs of slavery, and drinking four cups of wine, each a stage on 'the long walk to freedom', as Nelson Mandela called it. That narrative, as the great political philosopher Michael Walzer has pointed out, has been the inspiration for nearly every revolutionary political movement to liberate people from tyranny and slavery in the West.

By insisting on counting the days from Passover to Pentecost, however, we are making a statement that Passover was only the beginning of the journey, not the end. The culmination came several weeks later when the Israelites stood at the foot of Mount Sinai and accepted the covenant of the Ten Commandments and many others besides. For the first time, they became a body politic with a written constitution (the Torah, the Mosaic books of the Hebrew Bible) whose sovereign was God himself. Thus they were transformed from a collection of free individuals into a free society.

I want to explain why this second stage is necessary in Jewish thought. There is a difference between a free individual and a free society. As an individual, my freedom can easily conflict with yours. If I am free to steal, then you are not free to own property. If I am free to murder, then you are not free to live. If I am free to exploit, then you may only be free to be exploited. A society bounded only by free individuals freely associated with one another can easily become the rule of the powerful over the powerless. Judaism, on the other hand, insists that God is not on the side of the powerful, but on the side of the powerless. Judaism therefore proposes a simple alternative – not the rule of power, but the rule of law, in which each person has equal status, equal dignity, equal access to justice. It is highly significant that, at the covenant-giving on Mount Sinai, God appears not to an elite, not even to an individual, a prophet or a Son of God, but to an entire people, each of whom is a citizen in the republic created by that covenant.

Judaism has two words for freedom: *Hofesh* and *Herut*. *Hofesh* means freedom in the sense that I am not subject to anyone else's will, I am not a slave. That is what the Israelites achieved on Passover. *Herut* is different. *Herut* means collective freedom in a society in which I am free and you are free, and my freedom does not conflict with yours. That society can only come about when there is a shared moral code, when we practise self-imposed restraints, so that my liberties shall not be purchased at the expense of yours, and the powerful shall not rule over the powerless.

Last December I had the very sad task of officiating at the funeral of an extremely great man, the late Sir Isaiah Berlin of blessed memory. Isaiah was a dear friend, a fine Jew, but he and I disagreed about a number of things. He always used to say to me, 'Chief Rabbi, don't speak to me about God. When it comes to religion, I am tone deaf.'

He used to say to me, 'What I don't understand about you is how you studied philosophy at Oxford and Cambridge and yet you can still believe!'

I told him, 'Sir Isaiah, if it helps, think of me as a lapsed heretic.'

Sir Isaiah gave us possibly the most influential twentieth-century account of freedom that there is, the very famous essay called 'Two Concepts of Liberty'. In that essay he argued in favour of what he called 'negative liberty', i.e. all that matters is that I should be free from being constrained by somebody else, by some external power. Any attempt to give liberty a positive content would, he thought, result in totalitarianism.

Surely he was right to say that in an age still reeling from the Holocaust, the Third Reich and Stalin's communism, where the great threat to freedom was totalitarianism. Fifty years on, however, my own view as a Jew is that this is not the only threat. There is another threat to freedom which comes from the opposite direction, namely when a society lacks a shared moral code; when we begin to believe that there is no such thing as an objective moral order; when we think that morality is subjective, relative, or whatever I choose.

That is when societies begin to disintegrate from within. As happened in ancient Greece, ancient Rome and Renaissance Italy, we begin to see certain patterns: social pathology, social breakdown, a rise in crime, sporadic violence, depressive illness, social exclusion. There is less and less that holds us together as a society. We find it difficult to understand what it means to get together collectively, electively to pursue the 'common good'.

So I believe Sir Isaiah only gave us half the picture. On Passover the Israelites achieved negative liberty – they were free from slavery. Yet they could not *sustain* freedom without the second move, that of Pentecost, when they accepted a moral code to be internalized – whereby I limit my own actions to create space for you to enjoy the same public goods as I do. There is such a thing as positive liberty as well as negative liberty, and it exists in a society governed by a shared moral code.

That is my first point. In Jewish towns a free society must be a moral society. You cannot define citizenship, as Plato and Aristotle do, simply in terms of the arts of ruling and being ruled, i.e. being in a relationship of power. You have also to factor in the principle that to be a citizen is to be a free and equal participant in the moral enterprise, and that can only happen when we share certain values. That is why I gave such strong support to both the previous and the present Government, in their insistence that morality should be part of the national curriculum, and should indeed form the very essence of the ethos of schools.

People at the time said to the School's Curriculum and Assessment Authority, and to Nicholas Tate, who undertook the project, that it was impossible – that in a society like ours you could never get any agreement, any consensus, on what our shared moral code actually is. In fact, the truth is exactly the opposite. A total of 150 people were consulted from all faith communities, and they very rapidly reached a consensus (with one salient exception on how family should be taught in schools, and that, I believe, is part of a Judaic or Judaeo-Christian ethic) that a free society must be a moral society and one that teaches its morality to its children.

Now I want to explore one word, which I have used already and which is very significant. That is the word 'covenant', *brit* in Hebrew, and it is essential to Jewish thought. I want to go right back to the beginning, to the beginning of the Bible, when God created everything. You may remember that Genesis Chapter 1 is structured in a very striking way: 'And God said, "Let there be…" and there was… and God saw that it was good.' Again and again in Genesis Chapter 1 you see the words, 'And God saw that it was good.'

What is the first thing that the Bible calls 'not good'? 'It is not good for man to be alone.' Here is the crux of the political dilemma. On the one hand (and probably its most important contribution to human civilization), the Bible begins with the dignity of the human individual, made in the image of God. On the other hand, it also speaks of the limits of the individual: none of us is capable of living alone. We therefore seek association, we form ourselves into groups, and this is the essence of the political situation. The only trouble, the Bible tells us (and as anyone who lives in the Jewish community certainly knows), is that, however hard it is to live alone, it is also very hard to live together! With Adam and Eve comes conflict, with Cain and Abel comes fratricide, and before we have even reached the advertisements, the world is filled with violence in the days of the flood.

That is the typical Jewish situation. I am always amused by the story of the Rabbi who, on the holiest night of the Jewish year, the Day of Atonement, when all disagreements have to be terminated, decided that this year, on that night, he would get two members of his synagogue finally to make peace with one another. They had not spoken for 25 years. He spoke to each of them individually, and persuaded them to come together in the centre of the synagogue and shake hands after all this time. They shook hands, and the first one said to the second, 'I wish you all that you wish me.' Then the second one said, 'You see, Rabbi, again he's starting with me!'

The political question is, therefore, how do we learn to live together? I want to tell you two very different stories concerning this.

The first one, which has dominated Western thought since the seventeenth century, owes its genesis to a very significant political thinker called Thomas Hobbes, author of one of the most important political works of all time, the *Leviathan*. He asked the question: Why is it that people group together to form nations and states? He said that none of us can live alone for the obvious reason that, no matter how strong we are, we cannot defend ourselves against all possible attack. If there are no rules, if violence is permitted, none of us is safe, none of us has a guaranteed life. Therefore it is in each of our interests not to be in a state of nature, in a state without rules – what he famously described as life being 'nasty, brutish and short'. It is in each of our interests to delegate certain of our rights and certain of our powers to a central authority, which will monopolize power and will then be able to impose and police a set of laws, thus bringing about social order. We all gain from that situation, and that is why we create states – why we give away some of our freedom of action and say it belongs within the central body, within the Leviathan of the State. That is the key argument of what has come to be known as the 'social contract', the reason for the existence of states.

It is a famous story, but it is worth noticing a number of things about it. Firstly, who is the hero of Hobbes' story? Who is the leading character? The obvious answer is that the leading character is the 'I', the self, the lonely individual searching for the 'safe'. Secondly, what is his or her motivation in agreeing to the State? The answer is: rational self-interest. It is in my interests to be protected against somebody else by giving away some of my power to a government. Thirdly, the central drama in Hobbes' story is conflict. If we did not have a State, we would have conflict, an inevitable clash. While I pursue my interests, you pursue yours. Fourthly, that conflict is resolved by the centralization within the State of the legitimate use of power. What Hobbes has given us is an account of the institutions of State. The State is seen as an external imposition of order through a social *contract*, and individuals give up their power to the State. That is the famous Hobbesian story.

There is another story, however, and that is the story of the Bible itself. What happens after God says that it is not good for man to be alone? Well, man wakes up and finds that he is married. That is very interesting. He goes to sleep alone, and then he wakes up and sees 'wife'. In the first poem of the Bible, he says, 'This time I have found bone of my bone, flesh of my flesh; this shall be called 'woman' because she is taken from man.'

Incidentally, I should point out certain nuances here. Translated into English, it sounds like a chauvinistic proposition, but I want to point out a nuance which you can only read in Hebrew and not in English. Hebrew has two words for man: *Adam* and *Ish*. Until now, Adam has been called just that, *Adam*, which means 'man' in the sense of biological member of the species *homo sapiens*. This verse is the first time the Bible uses the name

Ish – in other words, man has to pronounce his wife's name, know her identity, before he even knows his own. He has to know the other before he knows himself. So for the Bible, the first institution of human association is not the State, it is marriage and the family. That, for the Bible, is the first of the political associations.

What is interesting is that the Bible takes it for granted that marriage is not a contract between two isolated individuals, each of whom is pursuing his or her own self-interests. This is not a contract, it is a *covenant*, a bond of love and identity – as Adam says, 'She is part of who I am.' In this case, the 'we' precedes the 'I'. This is central to the biblical view of society, namely that the key institution is the family and the key relationships are between husband and wife, parent and child, brother and sister.

How, for instance, does the Bible define its welfare legislation in the Book of Leviticus Chapter 25? It says, 'If your brother becomes poor…' Of course, that is not like talking about your literal brother, it is using the word as a metaphor, and it is an important one. The Bible tells me that I am expected to help others, not because it is in my long-term rational self-interest to do so, but because those others are part of my extended family. Society is seen as an extended family. Also, because families can sometimes be inward-looking and look after themselves rather than others, the Bible extends this relationship even to people who are not like me, not of my faith, not of my race.

It is sometimes said that the most important verse in the Hebrew Bible is Leviticus 19:17, 'You shall love your neighbour as yourself.' In my humble view, however, that is not the most important verse in the Bible. The most important verse is the one that comes 17 verses later. If it had been heeded, there would have been no Holocaust. It says, 'You shall not afflict the stranger, but you shall love the stranger as yourself, because you were once a stranger in the land of Egypt.' In other words, the stranger, the person who is totally unlike me, is part of me because I once stood where he stands today. Therefore, just as I wished to be helped then, I must help the stranger now.

I want to contrast this story with the story of Hobbes. Firstly, in the biblical story the hero is not the 'I', the lonely individual – it is the 'we', the human group of which I am a part. In its most basic form this group is the family, then the community, then society, and then the strangers. Above all, it is 'we' not 'I'. Secondly, the key motivation in the Bible is not self-interest, it is covenantal love. What is covenantal love? It is the kind of relationship which exists between husband and wife, parent and child, brother and sister – the kindness and compassion which is the Jewish definition of citizenship, the beauty of helping others. I do not help because it is in my interest to do so; I help because 'we' are part of the same group.

Now you can begin to understand the difference between a covenant and a contract. A contract is something I enter into with somebody else because it is in his interests and my interests to form that contract. When it ceases to be in our interests, we can break the contract. A covenant is a much stronger relationship. It is like a marriage, or even like parenthood. It signals our willingness to stay loyal to somebody, even when it is not in our interests to do so; to stay faithful even in tough times, even when it is dangerous or against my interests to do so – because my relationship to you is part of who I am as a human being.

That is why we are entirely wrong to translate the Hebrew word *emunah* – the other key word of Judaism – as 'faith'. In Judaism that does not mean faith, it means faithfulness, loyalty, fidelity, keeping your word once you have given it. That is the key religious value of Judaism. That is the covenant into which the Israelites entered at Sinai, when they pledged their loyalty to God and to one another, so that – 'Each Jew is responsible for each other Jew.' All of us are members of an extended family.

Once we see the society as an extended family, we will no longer talk about what is in our interests or about doing things 'because we have to'. Further, we will see that the key institutions of society from a biblical point of view are not so much the State as the family, the community, the school where we hand all our traditions on to future generations – the small institutions where, face to face, we discover who we are, to whom we are connected and of what traditions we are a part. We will see that the maintenance of society in Judaism depends less on power and police, and more on the collective responsibility we feel and accept as members of the 'we' that includes the 'I'.

Interestingly enough, if you look through history at how things turned out, you will see that the whole of Greek political theory (Plato, Aristotle) and the whole of European political theory (Hobbes, Locke) resulted in a series of nation states, city states, or even empires. By contrast, Judaism existed for almost 2,000 years – from the destruction of the Second Temple until the birth of the State of Israel – *without* a State. The Jews have survived as a society, as a series of self-governing communities throughout the world. Judaism, therefore, is about the maintenance of communities and societies, and not so much about the State.

It is inevitable, when you talk in terms of the State, that a key word is 'rights'. Why does the word 'rights' belong together with the word 'State'? Remember what Hobbes said: the State was only brought into being in order to guarantee me the right to life, the right to live in safety. For Locke it was the right to own property, it was freedom from theft. The State is there to protect certain things, and we call those things 'rights'. Rights are our claim, our legitimate claim, against the State.

It is equally inevitable, when we think in terms of the Judaic code of the society, the family, the community, that this word is not 'rights'. The key word here is 'responsibility', because the bond of mutual responsibility is exactly what a relationship is, as exists between a husband and a wife, between parents and children.

We have two ways of thinking about things, therefore: the State with its rights, and the community or the family with its responsibilities. It seems to me that you need both pictures, because a world without responsibilities, constructed entirely in terms of rights, generates conflicts that we cannot solve. Rights are absolute claims, so when they conflict there is nothing you can do. It is like being on a narrow road when there are two cars coming in opposite directions, with cars parked on both sides. There is only room for one to pass and neither of them is going to reverse. That is what happens in society when we talk only of rights.

The obvious example of this is the abortion argument as it appears in the States – between the right to life and the right to choose. Those are in a head-on conflict, one against abortion, one in favour, and there is no argument against either because rights are absolute claims. As Dworkin says, they are 'trumps' that over-ride every other card. In Judaism, however, the entire issue of abortion does not mention the word 'rights' at all, and it is a debate that has been going on for 2,000 years. It only mentions the word 'responsibility'. In Judaism we have a responsibility to protect the life and health of the mother, and we have a responsibility to protect the life of the unborn child. It is much easier to resolve conflicts of responsibilities than it is to resolve conflicts of rights.

In the case of abortion, our responsibility to the person who is actually there – the mother – takes precedence over our responsibility to the potential person who is not yet there, namely the foetus. Therefore, in Jewish law, we will commit abortion to save the life of, or prevent permanent damage to, the mother – but under no other circumstances. We have therefore resolved that issue, because it is easy to resolve clashes of responsibility, and impossible to resolve clashes of rights. When we have a society that thinks in terms of responsibilities, in terms not only of what we get from one another but also of what we give to one another, we are better able to resolve our moral disputes and far better able to live graciously together.

Let me summarize what I have been saying. There are two traditions which shape the liberal democracies of the West. One goes back to Plato and Aristotle, and on all the way through to

Hobbes and Locke and so on. It is primarily concerned with the State and political institutions. To be a citizen is to be involved with these institutions, to participate in the cut and thrust of political debate: citizenship has to do with issues of power, of ruling and being ruled.

The other tradition goes back to the Hebrew Bible, and is primarily concerned not with the State but with society and with the institutions that sustain society – the family, the community, the congregation, the school, the duties that we owe one another as part of the collective 'we'. To be a citizen under those terms is something different. It is not about ruling and being ruled, it is just about what it is 'to be' – to be a loyal spouse, a loyal parent, to be there when somebody else needs our help. That is a covenantal bond which has nothing to do with the social contract, nothing to do with self-interest, but everything to do with who I am and the group of which I am a part. It has less to do with rights and much more to do with responsibilities, namely the duties that I owe to those who are part of what I am.

These are the two traditions. They are not mutually exclusive: they are both true, and they both focus on different aspects of what it is to live together. However, for a long time we have focused almost exclusively on the State, and the reason we could do so was because those other institutions – the family and the community – could be taken for granted. They were strong, they were there, their existence could be taken for granted.

It is clear – to me at least, and surely to everyone by now – that we can no longer do this. While the State has grown stronger, families and communities have grown weaker and more fragmented. There is very little in Hobbes and Locke, or even in John Stuart Mill and Isaiah Berlin, about how to build and sustain families and communities. There is, instead, a great deal about the relationship between the individual and the State, about rights, about our freedom, and about the State leaving us alone to do what we like. I believe the time has come to think a little less about the State and a little more about society and community; about identity and belonging; about fidelity and trust; about mutual responsibility; about institutions like the family, where we learn what it is to share and where we learn what traditions we are a part of. It is time to think more about schools as the central institutions of society, as the place where one generation hands on its values to the next; and about freedom, not as the liberty to do what we like, but as the shared moral enterprise through which we work together to achieve what benefits us all.

As I began by saying, freedom is a journey, from Passover to Pentecost, from freedom as liberation to freedom as the collective exercise of moral responsibility. That is why, for me as a Jew, citizenship is so important and so central to our life, living graciously together.

GLADSTONE: A CONSUMMATE VICTORIAN CITIZEN

Roy Jenkins

20 OCTOBER 1998

Lord Jenkins of Hillhead is a Liberal Democrat Peer. He was formerly Home Secretary and Chancellor of the Exchequer (Labour) and was a co-founder of the Liberal Democrats in 1981. He is the Chancellor of Oxford University and the author of Gladstone.[1]

Gladstone was born in Rodney Street, Liverpool, in 1809 and died in Hawarden, North Wales – not very far away in miles, although across two estuaries, but very distinct in sociological terms. He died there in 1898, nearly 88 and a half years later. Liverpool remained Gladstone's base until he was about 20, but not Rodney Street. His father was rapidly becoming a rich man out of typical Liverpool trade in the early part of the nineteenth century: sugar, cotton and tobacco. He did not trade in slaves, even before the trade became illegal in Britain in 1807, but his West Indian plantations, like those of every other West Indian plantation owner, operated on slave labour. In 1815, when William Gladstone was five, John Gladstone disengaged from Rodney Street and moved about six miles down the Mersey to the rather grand Seaforth House, now demolished, which he had just completed building.

[1] R. Jenkins, *Gladstone* (London: Macmillan, 1995).

The Liverpool in which John Gladstone prospered, in which William Gladstone was born and passed his early life, the Liverpool of that period, was at the height of its burgeoning prosperity and explosive growth. It had already become a metropolis of ships and commerce with a high claim, which it maintained from 1790 to perhaps 1925, to be known as the second city of England. This was at a time when England was rapidly becoming the first country of the world. The Liverpool population in 1810 was 94,000, just below that of Manchester, Dublin, Glasgow and Edinburgh. It was, however, growing more rapidly and had more metropolitan quality about it than Manchester.

John Gladstone, who had been born in fairly humble circumstances and left school at the age of 13 in Scotland, was determined to make his sons into 'gentlemen', and he sent three of them to Eton. Only William, the youngest, made a real success of it. He carried off most of the prizes and had an even more successful Oxford career at Christ Church. There were always some, however, who doubted whether he had achieved the full gentlemanly status. Partly, of course, this was due to political partisanship towards the end of his career, but in mid-career there were always some Whig grandees, or perhaps even more their wives and daughters, who regarded him in a way slightly reminiscent of the attitudes of some of the grand Tories to Mrs Thatcher 20 years ago. That attitude was epitomized by somebody who said, 'There is something very middle class about the way Gladstone comes into a room.' I have no idea what that means, but it is interesting that it should have been said.

What is certainly the case is that he always retained a slight northern accent. There is a very early gramophone recording, a copy of which I possess, made, I think, in 1888. It is very scratchy, but there is no doubt that, although there is not a pronounced Scouse accent, there is a northern intonation, and not, in any case, a standard southern English accent. What is rather interesting and curious is that the old schools did not inculcate in their pupils in the first half of the nineteenth century a standard southern upper- or upper-middle-class speech. Peel, who was a Harrovian son of a Lancashire manufacturer even richer than John Gladstone, always spoke with a distinct Lancashire accent; and it was said of Addison, Winchester's only and not very distinguished Prime Minister, that he spoke with a burr, somewhere between a Hampshire yeoman and a Reading apothecary. Despite his great grandeur, Curzon, who was at Eton in the 1870s, was always famous for his short a's, as in 'brass and glass' on one famous occasion. It was really only the new public schools, founded after 1850 and following the pattern of Thomas Arnold's Rugby, which brought this standard southern English into the language. Whether that was a bad thing or a good thing, I do not know, but it was a curiosity and a fact which seems to be fairly well supported.

In the 1830s John Gladstone went back to Scotland, leaving the Liverpool in which he had done so well. He bought a fine estate, which is still in the possession of the family, and he lived the latter part of his long life there. That effectively severed William Gladstone's main connection with Liverpool. His second brother, Robertson Gladstone, remained in the city. He was an effective man of business, certainly in his early and middle life. He became Mayor of Liverpool before he was 40 years old and died in 1875 after a decade of decline. Gladstone himself always retained a certain nostalgia for Liverpool. Perhaps his most notable philosophical and theological address was delivered to Liverpool College in 1872, and he made the very last speech of his political life here, in the vast arena of Hengler's Circus, 18 months before he died. There was a satisfactory completion of the circle about that.

By this time he had become the most famous politician of the nineteenth century, and I want to turn now from Liverpool connections to his place amongst Prime Ministers, all 51 of them, from Walpole at the beginning of the first half of the eighteenth century, to Blair. Gladstone, in my view, may or may not have been the greatest Prime Minister. I hesitate only because he was never tested in a war for the country's survival, unlike the elder Pitt, the younger Pitt, Lloyd George and Churchill. He probably would not have been very good as a war leader, had he been faced with that prospect. What he was, without question, was the most remarkable specimen of humanity ever to be in No. 10 Downing Street, the most impressive animal who ever inhabited the forest of official London. Foremost of the qualities which gave him this pre-eminence was his energy; second, the breadth of his interests and activities; and third, the force and elevating quality of his oratory.

I would like to say a little about each of these qualities. His energy, both mental and physical, was phenomenal, both in its intensity during any one period and in its long-term persistence. It sustained him over a life span of 88 and a half years, much more unusual then than today, which included four separate Prime Ministerships. Gladstone is the only man to have been Prime Minister four separate times, the last of which ended only in his 85th year.

His intellectual qualities are illustrated by the breadth of his reading. The quantity of his reading becomes even more amazing because of its superimposition on his other activities, both intellectual and physical. He was obviously not just a remote bibliophile, sitting in his library from morning to night. He claimed that he read 20,000 books in the course of his adult lifetime – say the 70 years from 1825 when he was 16 to 1896 when he was 86 and his eyesight failed, so that he could not go on reading. A total of 20,000 is an extraordinary, almost unbelievable quantity of books to have got through. It means an average of 280 a year. Perhaps inspired by reading and writing about Gladstone, I, too, have taken to counting and keeping lists for the last five or six years. I read a moderate amount, and I find I read more now as I get older. It is one of the few benefits of old age that I need less sleep, and I wake up at about 5.30 in the morning and read for two hours. I have never succeeded in getting through more than 80 books in a year, however, but I am remarkably constant, never below 75, never above 85. Well, Gladstone did nearly four times that, alongside all the other things he did too.

Was his claim, therefore, of 20,000 just an idle boast? Politicians are supposed to be well-known boasters, and 20,000 is a good round number to think of, while 10,000 is perhaps not impressive enough and 30,000 too far over the top. But no, they are all listed in his diaries, and most of them are annotated in his unmistakable handwriting and can be seen in the St Deiniol's Residential Library of History and Theology in the village of Hawarden. The Library, to which he gave most of his books and to which he personally transferred them, pushing them in wheelbarrows along the approximately three-quarters of a mile from Hawarden Castle (the substantial mansion which belonged to his wife's brother and which he gradually took over), is still in the possession of his great-grandson. It would be a good subject for an allegorical painting entitled 'The Wheeling of the Books'. We can see the old man, then aged 86, pushing wheelbarrow after wheelbarrow of books along the long path.

Sometimes he gave the impression of just picking up any book which came his way and which increased his store of information. One example was Samuel Colt on the *Application of Machinery to the Manufacture of Rotating Chamber Barrel Firearms and their Peculiarities*, a subject in which he was not at all interested. This work, which was quite famous in his day, he perused for several hours, shortly before one of his early budgets as Chancellor of the Exchequer. He was, indeed, accused by Augustine Birrell, that great wit of the late nineteenth and early twentieth century, of reading for its own sake, pointlessly and frantically as though he was both running a race against time and trying to shut out disturbing reflections. Gladstone, he said, 'would rather read a second-rate book than think a first-rate thought'. This has always struck me as putting it rather foolishly, as though it were possible to order oneself to think a first-rate thought.

For the most part, however, there was more of a pattern to his reading. He read a great deal of theology and Church history. He was deeply involved in almost every liturgical and eschatological dispute, of which there were a great number in the middle years of the nineteenth century. He also wrote theology. Indeed, when he withdrew from the leadership of the Liberal Party after his first 1868–74 premiership, it was in order to devote himself, in what he thought were his declining years, to producing theological works. The trouble was that he was by no means a first-rate theologian, whereas he was indisputably a first-rate politician and statesman. As a result, almost as in the operation of a physical law, he was drawn back into what he was best at after 18 months and sustained his 'declining years' – which lasted for a quarter of a century – in being Prime Minister for another three times.

He was a better classical scholar than he was a theologian, although even here, while he had sound knowledge and muscular intelligence, he lacked the intuitive verbal sensitivity which marked out the greatest classicists. Nonetheless, he devoted a lot of time to classical texts. He read the Bible in Greek every day. He was devoted to Homer and published several commentaries on him, including some fairly fantastical theories which endeavoured to see him as part of the headwaters of Christianity. Towards the end of his life, work on his new translation of the *Odes* of Horace became a consuming passion. When he got back from Windsor after an ungrateful audience with Queen Victoria (on her side more than his) after he resigned for the last time as Prime Minister, he immediately got down to a Horace translation.

As a literary critic, his performance was somewhere between his theology and his classicism. He wrote a very good long essay on Tennyson, whom he also made the first and almost the only poet peer (Byron was hereditary). Although they knew each other nearly all their lives, Gladstone and Tennyson mostly circled around each other, rather like two cats with arched backs. Perhaps they were subconsciously aware that, together with only a handful of others – Cardinal Newman, Charles Dickens, Charles Darwin and perhaps Thomas Carlyle – they were two of the great stars of the nineteenth century, and as such needed their own, unimpeded orbits.

Gladstone also undoubtedly read more fiction, more novels, when he was in office than any subsequent British Prime Minister until Harold Macmillan. Macmillan read fiction which was contemporary to Gladstone rather than to himself, and he did so nearly a century later. Asquith would have run them both fairly close as a third contender. None of the other 48 Prime Ministers would have been anywhere near. Gladstone read all of the main Victorian novels as they came out: Trollope and George Eliot automatically, Dickens a little less enthusiastically, and many lesser ones as well. He also found time to go quite frequently back to Fanny Burney, Jane Austen and the Brontës. This, then, was the broad pattern of his reading.

I would like to give a few other examples of his energy before saying something about his oratory. I shall start with three physical examples, then finish with an intellectual one.

In 1883, when he was staying as minister in attendance with Queen Victoria at Balmoral, her Scottish Highland residence, he disappeared one day and, on a seven-and-a-half-hour round trip, climbed Ben Macdhui, at just over 4,000 feet the highest summit in the Cairngorms. It was not bad for a 74-year-old Prime Minister. He was no doubt keen to get away from the Queen, and she probably wanted to be free of him! (At this stage in their lives they did not get on, although they had got on earlier while Prince Albert was alive.) It was a strenuous means of attaining that end.

Later on, when Gladstone was just into his 80s, he was knocked down by a horse-drawn cab in London. He got up, pursued and overtook the driver and held him until the police came.

His favourite recreation in the second half of his life was felling trees – not bushes or shrubs, but great trunks. He went on doing this until a few weeks before his 82nd birthday. It is almost impossible to imagine any more strenuous exercise than hacking away with a heavy axe at a great and noble tree. He did not do it just in his own park either. Unless you possessed enough park-land, well wooded with a few redundant trunks, it was very dangerous to have Gladstone to stay.

Finally, here is an example of his intellectual rather than phys-ical energy. Right at the end of his last premiership, when he had been defeated in his second attempt to bring in Home Rule for Ireland, a tragedy for Anglo-Irish relations, and he was also in dispute about increased naval expenditure (which he was against) with all his Cabinet colleagues, nearly all of whom owed everything to him. In the midst of these huge problems he went to Brighton – he was very fond of Brighton – for a weekend. While he was there, he not only wrote out a draft of how he was going to denounce his colleagues at the Monday Cabinet meet-ing, as well as writing by hand his daily ration of about 15 long letters, but he also composed a 4,000-word essay on church music and how it had changed and improved during his lifetime. That was the essence of Gladstone. Nearly everybody else would have spent that weekend obsessed by grievance against his colleagues, or at least tried to avoid dwelling on it by playing golf (a bit early for that, maybe) or card games. Gladstone turned his mind in a totally different direction, but with opti-mism not bitterness.

Let us move on to his oratory, which was one of his greatest political weapons. That counted as a physical performance almost as much as an intellectual one. He established mass oratory as an art form, and very much a physical art form. The flash of his eagle eye, the swoop of his cadences, the drama of his gestures, were the physical attributes which made his speeches so riveting to large, popular audiences, despite their great length and convoluted language. At these large meetings he habitually spoke, not for about two and a half hours as in the House of Commons, but for one and a half to one and three-quarter hours.

At Edinburgh during the Midlothian campaign at the end of 1879, for instance, he spoke to a standing audience of 10,000 mostly 'working men', as they were then described, in the Waverley Market. He did so for one and three-quarter hours, and his speech was mostly made up of a complicated analysis and criticism of the Disraeli financial policy. Two questions arise in my mind: did they hear him, and, if they did, did they understand him? The answer to the first question, I have decided, is almost certainly 'no'. Reaching 10,000 people would be a most formidable feat for any voice entirely unassisted by amplification, and particularly so for a man of 70, as he was then, who had exhausted that organ over many decades of strenuous speaking.

This view was most strikingly supported for me in Edinburgh about three years ago when, after my address there on Gladstone, a very old man came up to me and said, 'My father used to be a shouter for Gladstone.' At first I could not think what he meant – I assumed just an enthusiastic cheerleader who, when he saw Gladstone in the street, shouted out 'Good old Gladstone!' But no, it was much more precise than that. Enquiry elucidated that, as a young man, his father was employed with others to stand maybe 25 or 30 yards back from the platform and then to turn round and shout a summary of Gladstone's discourse to the outer rim: 'He's going on to Bulgarian atrocities now!'

Was he understood? Compared with Lloyd George, the next great spontaneous orator who came after him, Gladstone elevated the interests and, with them, the self-esteem of his audiences. I think that this, combined with his extraordinary physical presence, accounts for the fact that, even if imperfectly heard, even if imperfectly understood because of the complication of his argument, he held these great audiences so that they went away satisfied and came back time and time again for more. He raised their self-esteem. He treated them as a grand jury of the nation. There is a very specific example of this in the speech he gave at the end of his Midlothian campaign. In West Calder he said, 'Here we have no bewigged judges as in Westminster Hall, we have no Lord Chancellor sitting on the Woolsack, but we are an even more important judge of the honour of England [you wouldn't get away with that in West Calder today, but that's what he said!] than any of these great dignitaries of state, because we are the jury of the nation.' As a result, he sent his audiences away thinking better of themselves than they had done when they arrived. As self-esteem is of great importance to nearly all of humanity, they went away fully satisfied and that, I believe, was a core part of the remarkable power and success of his oratory.

So what is my summing up? I was very hesitant about undertaking a book on Gladstone. I thought he was so much the highest peak in the mountain chain, he touched life at so many different points, that I was very hesitant about whether I could manage it. Once I started, however, I never regretted it. Although my admiration for Gladstone increased rather than diminished as I went along, I also found him to some extent a figure of fun and found it increasingly easy to laugh at him. I was aware at once of affection, admiration and amusement. I think that most really great men reveal elements of being figures of fun. Certainly Churchill did, certainly General de Gaulle did, and so did Gladstone. Very great men have a certain indifference to other people laughing at them and a certain indifference to possible ridicule which makes them very good figures of fun.

Gladstone himself was by no means lacking in humour. He had a considerable sense of rather boisterous fun, but little or no irony, and this quality perhaps gave him one of his strengths, which was no fear of ridicule. His wife of nearly 60 years, who nonetheless remains a somewhat shadowy figure in his otherwise very full and explicit diaries, made what I think is a very good remark about him after 25 of those 60 years. Many people thought he was too earnest to be easy to deal with. 'Oh, William dear,' she is reported to have said, 'if you were not such a very great man, what a bore you would be!' I find that remark much to her credit.

I did not find Gladstone a bore, despite his great earnestness. He had too much star quality for that, and it infused almost everything he did with a touch of magic. At any rate, he held my interest throughout my years of work on him, and I hope that I have to some extent engaged your interest in him too.

COMPLEX QUESTIONS FOR IRELAND

Mary McAleese

24 NOVEMBER 1998

Mary McAleese is the President of Ireland. She was formerly a barrister and the Director of the Institute of Legal Studies and Pro Vice-Chancellor of Queen's University, Belfast.

The concept of citizenship, or of being a citizen, is something which you generally take for granted, because you have grown up with it and live it every day of your life. When I was asked to talk about it, my first inclination was to reach for the dictionary for a formal definition of precisely what it means. In my diction- ary the definition of 'citizen' is 'an inhabitant of a city; a member of a state; a townsman; a freeman; a civilian'. Straight away I knew I had some work to do, even if only to update the definition in terms of gender balance! The *lived* experience of being a citi- zen is, of course, something a lot more than those few words in the dictionary can encompass. The complexities of living as a citizen are very different from any principled definition of citi- zenship, because the concept touches people in the most passionate of places: where their identity, their sense of who they are, their sense of belonging, their sense of worth and their sense of value all merge – or do not, as the case may be.

As a person who came from a place where there was a very complex set of issues to do with citizenship, my starting point is my own experience. I was born in Belfast, an Irish person born into an Irish nationalist background, with a very strong sense of identity with the south of Ireland – where the constitution recognized my citizenship of Ireland but did not confer any voting rights on me whenever I went to stand for election because I lived north of the border. In the place where I had a vote – in Northern Ireland – although I was a citizen, there was a feeling that my full citizenship was always an issue. My teenage years coincided with the civil rights movement, which drew attention to the many aspects of full citizenship that were denied to Catholics in Northern Ireland.

Issues to do with citizenship and identity are very often at the heart of some of the more intractable conflicts in our world. Getting those relationships right between the individual and the place in which they are going to live their lives – and the structures that are built up around it – is crucial. In the past, the accepted citizenship model in which I was expected to live was an old conflict model. You could only be one thing or the other – Irish or British, Irish or European, British or European. Life was built around tight and exclusive choices. The notion of parallel, twin and even triple identities was anathema, yet these identities were part of my own personhood and the crude choices shaped a particular understanding of ourselves, our history and our times.

Yet the Irish have shown that you can be a citizen of Ireland, a citizen of Europe. Our global outreach has made us natural citizens of the world. We are a people who are particularly well placed to talk about citizenship, because our gift to the world for centuries has been our people. We are 70 million right across the globe today. If we go back into another millennium entirely, long before the word 'global' was ever thought of, we were citizens of the world. While other countries endured a Dark Age, there never was such an age in Ireland. Indeed, at the point at which England was enduring its Dark Age, we were experiencing one of our greatest cultural highlights. We were interconnecting with the Viking world, with the world of Islam, and in that sense, we were outreaching to the world. So this quirkiness today, which sees us almost in a 'Reformation time warp', is certainly part of our present – part of the colonial legacy – but we are building on and rediscovering a very ancient tradition, a very ancient set of sources which are helping us in a very profound way to craft a new future of citizenship.

We know, for example, that there are big issues in Britain to do with citizenship of Europe and citizenship of Britain. Indeed, the old Empire had its problems too – people who were part of the far-flung Empire and who thought of themselves as British citizens found, when they went to assert their British citizenship, that it was often problematic and did not confer the entitlements they had presumed. The lived experience of citizenship is extra-ordinarily tangled – however, it does repay untangling.

Over the last two months, I have been on State visits to Australia and Canada, my first since coming to office just over a year ago. In both countries (or the 'new countries', as they were once known) I met with communities and individuals who cher-ished their links with their ancestral homelands, who were proud to celebrate their inherited cultures and traditions. Yet they were also participating fully, with pride, enthusiasm and in a great many cases considerable levels of success, in the economic, political and cultural lives of their 'adoptive' countries. What struck me also was the comparative ease with which they were able to live and prosper side by side with others from different traditions and cultures, and at times even with former foes.

In the case of those who emigrated from Ireland, with the exception of the very recent emigrants, the vast bulk of those 70 million who comprise the global Irish family are first- or subse-quent-generation descendants of those who were persuaded (or even compelled) to leave Ireland because they endured a form of 'stunted citizenship', where the 'common interest' did not encompass their needs or did not adequately provide the means and mechanisms for them to meet their needs. They were excluded from real participation in the economic and social life of their native country, which in turn inhibited their involvement in the societies in which they lived. Their citizenship of their natural land did not confer political, social or economic opportunities, never mind equality. Their giftedness remained locked in. In contrast to that experience, they were to blossom and flourish in the 'new world' – as if to prove that they were just as capable as anybody else at the task of building a viable and sustainable society that rewarded enterprise and cherished a broader concept of the common interest.

Their successes were largely facilitated by the culture of opportunity, and by the imperative of building new societies based on the principles of liberalism which prevailed in the eighteenth century especially, exemplified in the writings of Rousseau, and which spawned the revolutionary movements in places like France and America. Indeed, that revolutionary spirit was echoed in Ireland in 1798, when the United Irishmen drew on events in America and France for inspiration and promoted the ideal of nonsectarian, democratic and inclusive politics which could attract and sustain all Irish people, with all their inherited complexities. Rather than grimly clinging to a divisive past, they sought to create a shared future. As they stated in their first declaration of principle, 'We have thought much about our posterity, little about our ancestors.' In that process they were to succeed in uniting Dissenter, Anglican and Catholic in a common political mission. It is not entirely without significance in this momentous year in Ireland's recent history – a year in which we have seen a major step forward in reconciling long-held differences and divisions – that we should reflect on the ideals and aspirations of those people of 200 years ago, who tried to bring hearts and minds together in the common cause of a new citizenship for all the people of Ireland, regardless of creed or tradition.

Rousseau's concept of the state was that it should be capable of forming a general will for the common good. 'It is one of the most important functions of government to prevent extreme inequality of fortunes,' he wrote. Rousseau and others who have been exercised by the concept of citizenship since the time of Aristotle have provided us with varying definitions of citizenship. Each was moulded by the prevailing circumstances and in some cases drew on earlier and ancient definitions; each was pertinent in its relevance to bringing order out of the 'chaos' which then obtained; and each was subject to definition and redefinition as circumstances changed.

The Greeks, for example, were concerned with smaller city-states riven with conflict between rich and poor and by wars with neighbouring states, but they felt (in their wisdom) that citizenship was not possible in Persia because 'excessive heat made men supine and ready for despotism', and that it was equally impossible in the colder northern countries because 'excessive cold' meant that people were limited to basic survival.

As we know, citizenship was to flourish in republican Rome, which enjoyed a mixed government made up of princedom, aristocracy and populace, where all three had their share, and where liberties were safeguarded by a continuous tension between the senate and the people. As Machiavelli put it, 'The aspirations of free people are seldom harmful to liberty, because they result either from oppression or from fear that there is going to be oppression.'

Whatever the type of citizenship that prevailed in the different ages, the underlying rationale for the concept of a political community was to bring order into society, in place of chaos or caprice. With the passage of time and the ebb and flow of history, citizenship has developed and altered to reflect contemporary concepts of the 'common good' and its balance with the interests of groups and individuals. Machiavelli believed that there was a cyclical nature to governments, with bad governments being replaced by citizens who 'conducted themselves according to the laws they laid down, subordinating all of their advantage to the common good, and with the greatest diligence cared for and preserved things private and public' – only to be followed by a succeeding generation who, 'refusing to content themselves with equality ... but turning to avarice, to ambition, to violence against women, caused a government of the best of men to become a government by the few, without having regard to civil rights'.

The twentieth century has seen the turbulence of two world wars and other serious conflicts. There has been massive disloca- tion of peoples, with all that implies for the undermining of citizenship and the rights that go with it. Thankfully, the twenti- eth century has also seen a serious discourse on human rights, and we are now celebrating the fiftieth anniversary of the UN Declaration of Human Rights. The Declaration does not confer rights, but simply enumerates the God-given rights of the person and provides a vehicle for vindicating them and ensuring that governments honour them. It gives us hope that the twenty- first century will show more evidence of the sacredness of the human person which lies at the heart of true citizenship. That sense of the sacred, that sense of respect, is what matters for contented citizens. Where there is serious discontent, that respect is usually absent.

For Ireland, circumstances in the 1840s saw a population decimated by the Great Famine, while food producers were allowed to export with the support of a government that did little to alleviate the desperate plight of the population. Citizenship was a hollow concept for those who bore the brunt of the suffer- ing. For them there was no recognition that famine was a threat to the common interest. Famine was not considered to be a threat to the particular 'society' in which officialdom had an interest and on which it focused. The victims were therefore not considered to be 'participating' citizens and were left without a sense of belonging to the political community – a feeling of inclusion and respect that is an essential prerequisite for active citizenship. So, while they were Irish nationals and 'citizens' of a part of the British Empire, they could not subscribe to the accepted establishment view of what constituted the common good. They were alienated. In the words of the Prime Minister,

Tony Blair, 'Those who governed in London at the time failed their people through standing by while a crop failure turned into a massive human tragedy … That one million people should have died in what was then part of the richest and most powerful nation in the world is something that still causes pain as we reflect on it today.'

In the century and a half since the Great Famine, there have been profound changes in political structures throughout the world, especially in the decades which followed the First World War. Those changes, which have seen the spread of democracy and a greater level of inclusion, have in turn brought the concept of citizenship to new levels. With the higher concentration of populations in cities, and the need to redefine the concept of community, the definition of what constitutes the 'common good' has had to be continually honed and recrafted to fit the new order. In places where there were attempts to confine the domain of citizenship to select groups, or to pursue sectional interests by limiting access to full participation, a conflict has eventually ensued. In South Africa, where a regime of apartheid saw the majority of the population living a scaled-down version of citizenship, it was inevitable that sooner or later they would react as they did – and come to a new level of political community where the common good embraces all. In Northern Ireland, the decades-long exclusion of the Catholic minority from the mainstream of civic life led inevitably to frustration, and the scene was set for political instability.

Still today, in parts of Eastern Europe, we see history sadly repeating itself, with one group trying to subjugate another and to impose their own narrow definition of citizenship, which sees the interests of the others relegated to second place or even excised completely. What is shocking and sickening to most people is that we have seen ethnic cleansing used yet again in the twentieth century as a means to 'limit the pool' to those who can comfortably live with the new and blinkered definition of the 'common interest'.

Over the last decade in Ireland we have seen tremendous economic and demographic changes – changes that have brought prosperity and opportunity to many, and changes that represent challenges to individuals and communities. These recent developments have come about in large part because of our joining with our European neighbours 25 years ago. This was an event which forced us to look outward rather than inward, and one which has seen a broadening of horizons and a widening of our definitions of what constitutes the common interest. In the field of gender equality, the last quarter of a century has seen many barriers being dismantled and many obstacles to full participation being removed – at times only reluctantly and under duress. Nonetheless, the pace of progress has been relentless and it has surely been brought about by the widening definition of the common interest, through our association with our European partners. We have been compelled to look beyond our own parish and town to other places and other people with differing values and differing concepts of citizenship.

In Ireland, as elsewhere, these changes have precipitated an examination of where we are in relation to local, national and European institutions. The shift of administrative focus to Europe, and the concern that the interests of individuals and communities may be subsumed into a new, homogenized European identity, has in a way rekindled the concept of the local citizen, of being part of a unique place with its own cultures and traditions. Paradoxically, our very membership in Europe has sharpened and refreshed our sense of identity so that we have lived to see the truth of Professor Tom Kettle's words, written 80 years ago before he died at the Somme: 'Ireland will only find her deep identity when first she embraces Europe.'

In Ireland we have seen how this has led to a growth in local, community-based structures and partnerships which are adding a new and exciting dimension to the concept of citizenship. Local people have taken ownership of their communities and their problems, and are working with statutory and voluntary bodies to address these as they see fit and in accordance with the community's definition of their common interest. We have reached a new level of community empowerment. While some may argue there is a danger that the narrow focus and limited participation in these local partnerships can lead to the domination of sectional interests, the mechanisms are there at county and national levels to ensure that the wider public interest is not detrimentally affected.

With all the progress that we have made, however, there are still matters to be addressed; there are still things to be put right. None of us can afford to be smug and to say that the problems of exclusion and marginalization are problems for somebody else 'over there' and away from our healthy society. In practically every society there are those who are marginalized, who are not embraced as full citizens enjoying full participation and recognition. While the numbers involved may be small – and therefore not posing an enormous threat to the communities in which they live – their confinement as a separate, deliberately excluded group is fundamentally wrong and unhealthy, and it holds the potential for future instability.

Even in the most advanced societies there is never room for complacency. There is a need constantly to review and critique how society is working, how it is using the talents and skills of its citizens, and how it is enabling its citizens to participate. Citizenship does not necessarily embrace the way you feel about a place. There can be processes that alienate. We need to have sensitive ears and sensitive fingertips at the policy-making level. We need people in positions of leadership whose ears are attuned to those sensitivities and who can draw in the strands of disaffected citizens in order to give them that real spirit of citizenship. To be a citizen does not necessarily mean that you have that spirit of citizenship, but to live without it is to live in a twilight, a place of limbo, and to see your gifts used only partly, badly, or not at all.

Northern Ireland has seen 30 years of conflict, and for decades before that had followed the limited citizenship model I described earlier, which contained the seeds of its own demise. This year, however, we have seen a new departure with the Good Friday Agreement, which was overwhelmingly endorsed by the people, releasing into the dynamic of politics a huge, new and energetic empowerment. People decided individually to commit to a painful process of change, in which there would be winners and winners, not winners and losers. The old culture of conflict has given way to the building of a new culture of consensus. These exciting new developments are opening up that concept of citizenship where all citizens of the island of Ireland will have a sense of ownership and citizenship of their place. The Good Friday Agreement, and the 'yes-ness' that was exhibited in the referenda that endorsed it, has given all of us hope for the future – the hope that citizenship is a concept that helps us to transcend difference: not to obliterate difference, but simply to transcend it.

In developing our new concept of a citizenship of Ireland, we are very grateful for the help we have received from the global Irish family. Whether through their words of encouragement or through their prayers, all of them have in their own way given the process the push that it needed. We are grateful, too, for the support and encouragement we have received from people throughout the world who have willed us on.

As I said earlier, we are building on a very ancient tradition, a very ancient set of sources which are helping us in a very profound way to craft a new future of citizenship. We have reached a new plane in the spiral of history from which we can move forward with new perspectives. New relationships with our island neighbour are the reward of untangling the chaos of our complex identity, our skewed concepts of citizenship. A new, mature and comfortable citizenship is on offer to all. Hopefully we will soon have something very profound to say to the rest of the world about citizenship.

THE CONSERVATIVE SAMARITAN

Ann Widdecombe

29 JANUARY 1999

The Rt Hon. Ann Widdecombe is the Conservative Member of Parliament for Maidstone. She was formerly Minister of State at the Home Office (1995–7), and is currently the Shadow Home Secretary.

Individual responsibility and the willingness of each of us to play our full part in the society in which we find ourselves are increasingly important. We all have duties and responsibilities as well as rights and it is appropriate that, from time to time, we should concentrate on these. It has become increasingly fashionable to expect the 'State' to cope with every problem and it is too easy for a feeling to grow up that as soon as we have paid our taxes we have discharged our responsibilities, whereas each of us has responsibilities to our fellow men and women over and above any fiscal contribution which we might make.

I should like first of all to consider the parable of the Good Samaritan. The parable is well known beyond the confines of the Christian Church, and the phrase 'the Good Samaritan' has entered common parlance. I derive my ideas of citizenship directly from this parable, so let me rehearse once more the main features of the story.

A man went on a very long journey – in those days such journeys were often made on foot and could take days or weeks. He was travelling between one town and another when he was set on by thieves. In modern parlance, he was mugged and battered and then left to take his chance by the wayside. Two pillars of the local community then came along, saw his plight, but simply kept going – or, as the Authorized Version puts it, 'they passed by on the other side', another phrase which has become a commonly used metaphor in the English language. Eventually a Samaritan came along, saw the man suffering, tended to his wounds, set him on his own beast (as the Authorized Version picturesquely describes it), took him to an inn and left him in the care of the innkeeper, paid for his immediate keep and promised that, if the sum should prove insufficient, when he next passed the same way he would make it up to the right amount.

The traditional interpretation of this parable is a warning against snobbery and exclusion, as Samaritans were despised by the inhabitants of Jerusalem. The story is often portrayed as emphasizing that people on whom you look down can in fact be the people on whom you ultimately have to rely. Conversely, people on whom you should be able to rely very often simply pass by on the other side. However, there is much more to it than that and in that short and simple parable I see a clear blueprint for the way a State should be run and the individuals in it discharge their duty of citizenship. I believe it gives us the key to good citizenship in the single word 'trust'.

Let us now look at this parable in more detail. First of all, we are taught what the priorities of both the State, as an organization, and the individual citizens within it should be. The Samaritan put the man by the wayside first because he was in great and pressing need. We must, however, assume that the Samaritan was passing that way on purposes of his own, i.e. he had some business, either commercial or personal, which needed his attention. The Samaritan, however, stopped in his tracks, postponed whatever the business was which up to that moment had been claiming his attention, and instead focused on someone in greater need. That is a blueprint for how we can be good citizens. It is no good being so intent on our own purposes, however legitimate, if we ignore the more pressing claims of compassion and humanity. The Samaritan allowed the claims of compassion to over-ride the claims of his everyday business. There are lessons here, both for the individual citizen and for the State.

We often think that, in order to be compassionate, we have to go looking for suffering, but very often it is there in the course of our everyday lives and it can claim us at very inconvenient moments. When I address school speech days, which is quite often now, I always point out that the person in need may be not only the famine victim in a far-off country, but the student next door in a hall of residence, or the person at the next desk at school. Nor can we put compassion into specified parts of our timetable and say, 'Ah, on Tuesday night I will visit the sick.' We have to allow it to interrupt our normal business, to take first claim on our duty. The lesson is similar for the State. The State also has a duty to provide, if you like, organized compassion. It has to run health services, pension systems, education systems, social security systems, social services, etc. These have legitimate claims on any State's priority when it comes to spending. It is no good a State simply seeking to become wealthy if it does not have a very clear purpose for the use of that wealth.

There are many by the wayside in our society. Sick people are by the wayside; homeless people are by the wayside; pensioners wondering how to stretch out their pensions are by the wayside; people in prison facing imminent release without adequate preparation are by the wayside. The list goes on. Neither as individuals nor as an organized society can we pass by on the other side.

We also learn from this parable, however, the importance of creating wealth. When anybody asks me how on earth I can be a Conservative and a Christian, I always say, 'Look at the parable of the Good Samaritan.' After all, the Samaritan had to have the money to pay the innkeeper. If he had not had the money to pay the innkeeper, he could not have arranged for the victim's care after he himself moved off the scene. Even before he paid the innkeeper, however, he was using his personal wealth for the benefit of his fellow human being. What a good job it was, from the point of view of the victim, that the Good Samaritan was not making a journey on foot. Rather, he was travelling with a beast and he put that beast at the service of the victim and used it to transport him to the inn. Occasionally you will hear people say, 'Why have cars when you can make do with pedal cycles?' But just imagine trying to transport somebody to hospital on a pedal cycle.

There is nothing wrong, therefore, with the accumulation of wealth and with obtaining consumer goods – these days a car, in those days a beast – if those goods are used for the benefit of our fellow human beings as well as for our own convenience. The Samaritan started off quite legitimately with his beast, but when he could also put it to the service of his fellow man, that is what he did. Furthermore, we learn in that parable that he used wine and oil and cloth to bind up the wounds of the one who had fallen among thieves. So he was well provided for. One may assume, perhaps, that he was a successful small businessman, and the profits had a use in addition to his own convenience.

The same lesson is there for the State. The State also has to pay the innkeeper. Capitalism is the system which ensures that a State can pay the innkeeper. Health services have to be paid for, pension systems have to be paid for, social services have to be paid for, and anything else that is done to promote health and wellbeing. They cannot be paid for through goodwill and good intentions alone. Society has to be able to pay the innkeepers of these services. That is why the enterprise culture and the acquisition of wealth are in themselves essential to good citizenship. Indeed, the necessary acquisition of wealth by the State lays duties on us as citizens. First of all, we must pay, and take pride in paying, any taxes which are lawfully levied upon us – unless the State has made them excessive, in which case we must still pay, but perhaps without the pride. Tax evasion is not a game, it is a mark of very bad citizenship. It is, so to speak, robbing the innkeeper.

Of course, not everybody will contribute directly to a nation's wealth creation. Some, who supply services rather than creating trade or commerce, will draw on the very taxes that I have just been talking about. Yet they, and we who use their services, depend on the wealth creators to fund those services. We should never forget that. I believe that sometimes there is an erroneous view that those who serve directly or who have vocations rather than creating wealth are somehow morally superior. They are not. The innkeeper cannot be paid through moral superiority.

The real lesson of this parable is actually in its ending. The Samaritan could not stay, but left what he thought was a reasonable sum for the man's care and the provision of his needs. He promised the innkeeper that when he returned, if that sum was insufficient he would make up the difference. Everybody benefited from this simple act of trust. The Samaritan had to trust the innkeeper. He had to trust that the bill the innkeeper would eventually produce would not be a fictional one, that it would be a true representation of anything that had been spent. He had to trust the innkeeper not to throw the man out as soon as his back was turned and then to claim falsely for his care and the provision of his needs. The innkeeper also had to trust the Samaritan. He had to trust that he would pass that way again (and in those days that might have been some time off) and that, when he did pass that way again, he would honour his pledge to pay without haggling and without unreasonable argument.

Everybody benefited from this, as I said. The innkeeper benefited because he got the custom that he would not have been able to get if he had not been prepared to trust the Samaritan. The Samaritan benefited because he was able to go on about his business without any further interruption and with his conscience eased. Above all, the victim of the thieves benefited because his care was thoroughly provided for.

Today, trust is breaking down in our society. Indeed, one might say that it is already largely broken down. For example, I belong to a profession which is hardly trusted at all! Yet it is vital that society builds itself on trust, and that we build our notions of citizenship on the basis of trust. There has to be trust between rulers and those whom they rule. People have to believe that those to whom they entrust power will use it to the very best of their ability and in the best of faith. If not, if people do not believe that, then the democratic process must eventually break down and the role which individual citizens play in a democracy will become of decreasing importance. It is also necessary, however, that those who rule can trust the people to whom they give laws.

For example, if a State sets up a social security system, it must do so not only on the basis of a set of rules, but also on the basis of trust. It must be able to trust individual citizens not to abuse those rules. I said earlier that fiddling income tax was a mark of bad citizenship. So is fiddling social security. If people abuse the system, then other people suffer, because the resources of a State are not unlimited. In the end, in a reverse of the situation with the Samaritan and the innkeeper, we all suffer rather than benefit. The biggest sufferers are the innocent victims, who receive less generous benefit because it has to be spread more thinly and is not being used for the purpose for which it was originally designed.

It is therefore a duty of citizens not to abuse the systems which their rulers – particularly, but not exclusively, democratic rulers – set up specifically for the benefit of the needy. Let us bring trust now into a more domestic setting. Trust has broken down as an underlying concept, not only between people doing business but between people in more personal situations. We have recently had a spate of what the press like to deem 'revelations'. For example, we have had Margaret Cook, after decades of marriage, revealing the alleged weaknesses and practices of her former husband. The siblings of Jacqueline du Pré have also produced their recollections, which are not over-flattering to their subject. These days everybody, whether for fame, money or revenge, breaks confidences, breaks trust, reveals what was given in private. Wives tell, mistresses tell, royal courtiers tell, employees tell, political campaign managers tell, everybody tells. This cannot benefit anybody. Once again, in a reverse of the situation with the Good Samaritan, the absence of trust penalizes all involved. No man is an island, except in public. In public, we hide our weaknesses, our fears, our innermost selves. In private, we reveal these things on the basis of trust. When that breaks down, personal relationships themselves become superficial and are undermined by suspicion.

Our ancestors had a word for it. They did not talk about trust or integrity: they talked about 'honour'. That is the concept which has largely disappeared from our society. It was honour that bound a man to his wife, even when he was thoroughly fed up with the home. It was honour that kept a quarrelling couple together because they knew that their first duty was towards their children. It was honour that meant one paid one's taxes and did not make false declarations for the purposes of obtaining what we would now call social security, but would once have called national assistance and, even before that, the poor law. It was honour which also underlaid commerce. In those days, people did not sign agreements in triplicate. There is no mention that the innkeeper and the Good Samaritan sealed their bargain with their signatures. There was an understanding that a person's word was sufficient. It is a very long time now since business in this country was conducted on the basis of a person's word. When did you last go into a shop and have your cheque accepted without having to produce a guarantee card?

What I am trying to demonstrate is that the root of citizenship has to be the way that individual citizens relate to each other. Trust is the underlying factor which determines whether or not a society runs smoothly, runs soundly and runs securely. I think we need a major campaign to reinstate trust as the basis on which we deal with each other. The betrayal of trust always has a consequence beyond the parties concerned. These days there is a trade in the betrayal of trust stronger than the trade in sliced bread. The public lap up such betrayal. Newspapers and media make very considerable profits from it, but every time trust is betrayed a small – or sometimes large – erosion appears in the fabric of society. People become less willing to trust each other.

Let us look, for example, at the trust which is extended by the vulnerable towards professions. Let us consider the very extensive damage done by the case of the Bristol doctors and, indeed, other instances where negligence by professionals has been revealed. When trust in professionals breaks down, there is an increase in the sum of fear and doubt felt by those who have to place their trust in such people, and a sense of vulnerability and loss of reputation on the part of those who have had no direct role in the breach of trust, but who still feel tarnished by it.

Employers must be able to trust employees to work without direct supervision and to uphold the best interests of the company or organization in which they are employed. Employees must be able to trust employers that wages will be paid on time and properly. Trust, however, goes beyond those very narrow and possibly legal requirements. Trust also means one person being able to rely utterly on another. Hence, if the employee is ill, a good employer will do his best to look after the person and not merely regard the illness as an inconvenient debit in the ledger, taking up time and money. Similarly, the employer must be able to trust the employee that when there are particular needs, the employee will not simply rely on the precise wording of a contract, but will do his or her best to help the employer and the organization.

These may seem very obvious examples, but the widespread breach of trust – and the gradually growing assumption that it cannot be relied upon but rather must be enforced through complex legal agreements – reduces human relationships to an elaborate game of 'let me see what I can get away with' on one side, and 'I wonder what fast one they are trying to pull now' on the other side. Trust, as the foundation for building and developing citizenship, is often the ignored dimension. Its rediscovery on a personal, domestic, commercial, social and national scale would be a major impetus in building a society in which citizens care for and respect each other as a matter of course.

THE RESPONSIBLE CITIZEN

David Alton

10 FEBRUARY 1999

Lord Alton of Liverpool is an independent crossbench peer and Professor of Citizenship at Liverpool John Moores University. For 18 years he was a member of the House of Commons and before that served on the Liverpool City Council. He is the author of six books including Citizen Virtues[1] *(HarperCollins, 1999).*

Two short paragraphs, 42 and 43, in the White Paper *Excellence in Schools*, published in July 1997, announced the UK Government's intention to educate for citizenship:

> Schools can help to ensure that young people feel that they have a stake in our society and the community in which they live by teaching them the nature of democracy and the duties, responsibilities and rights of citizens.

How they will deliver this remains unclear – not least to the Government itself – which is perhaps why they then followed the time-honoured course of setting up an advisory group 'to discuss citizenship and the teaching of democracy in our schools'. (When in doubt, set up a committee.) The membership of that Committee will wield enormous influence in shaping an

[1] D. Alton, *Citizen Virtues* (London: HarperCollins, 1999).

agenda which cuts to the heart of how a person perceives his or her relationship with the wider community. It is foolish to under-estimate the high stakes involved as politicians seek to define citizenship.

The debate about 'educating for citizenship' has become a cipher for a more fundamental debate about philosophy and theology, relativism and absolutism, values and virtues, the indi-vidual and the community. Some are using it as a smoke screen to see off religious education and the daily act of worship in schools – which, in the light of the extraordinary outpouring of spontaneous, but frequently unstructured, religious feeling over the tragic death of Diana, Princess of Wales, is a lamentable response to a nation trying to find spiritual meaning to questions of mortality and immortality.

If all that emerges is a view of citizenship which encourages another series of miserable little charters, linked to consu-merism, choice, entitlements and rights, it will be another wasted opportunity. Nor should we contemplate a return to the mainly abandoned teaching of civics – a dreary litany of constitutional questions. If citizenship is merely taught as civics, it will be an empty cask drained of all its richness. Here, then, I would like to consider two things:

1 The circumstances which led to the 1997 Government White Paper.
2 The political and educational response.

The White Paper had its genesis in 1990, when Lord Weatherill, the former Speaker of the House of Commons, issued his report 'Encouraging Citizenship' (the report of the Commission on Citizenship). The Commission spawned the excellent Institute for Citizenship Studies, which works alongside other charitable bodies such as the Foundation for Citizenship.

The Secretary of State for Education, David Blunkett, was a member of the Weatherill Commission which declared that 'citizenship should be a part of every young person's education from the earliest years of schooling and continuing into the post-school years within further and higher education'. There is no reason to believe that anything which has happened since 1990 has changed David Blunkett's views. Quite the reverse.

The role of education in the formation of citizens became the central concern of Mrs Frances Lawrence following the tragic death of her husband, Philip, outside his London school. After the killing of James Bulger and the massacre at Dunblane, there was similar national introspection. However, the publication of Frances Lawrence's personal manifesto, David Selbourne's *The Principle of Duty*,[2] Amitai Etzioni's *The Spirit of Community*,[3] and Jonathan Sacks' *The Politics of Hope*[4] and his 1990 Reith lectures, all played a significant part in challenging the previous ortho-doxies of individualism and rights. In the latter Dr Sacks says, 'It is as if in the 1950s and 1960s we set a time bomb ticking which would eventually explode the moral framework into fragments. The human cost has been colossal.'[5]

In higher education, at the Centre for Philosophy and Public Affairs at St Andrews, at Leicester University and at the Liverpool John Moores University, significant work has been undertaken into values education and the development of citizenship. Profes-sor Peter Toyne, the former Vice Chancellor of Liverpool John Moores, has said that 'citizenship stems from the process of education'.[6] It has become the first university in the United King-dom to commit itself to developing a strong sense of citizenship among all of its 20,000 students.

That formal education should play its part in promoting the virtues of honesty, compassion, respect, responsibility and justice has also been recognized by Parliament and within the

[2] D. Selbourne, *The Principle of Duty* (London: Sinclair Stevenson, 1994).
[3] A. Etzioni, *The Spirit of the Community* (London: Fontana Press, 1995).
[4] J. Sacks, *The Politics of Hope* (London: Jonathan Cape, 1997).
[5] J. Sacks, *Faith in the Future* (London: Darton, Longman & Todd, 1995).
[6] P. Toyne, The Hockerill Lecture, 1995.

school inspection framework of the Office for Standards in Education (OFSTED), who are already required to give attention to spiritual, moral, social and cultural development. This has been further reflected in the establishment of the Values Education Council (VEC), and through the School Curriculum and Assessment Authority (SCAA) initiative in creating the National Forum for Values in Education and the Community. SCAA's much awaited statement on the promotion of values was published in 1998.

Nicholas Tate, its director, rightly asked what should be the 'ends' of education and whether the teaching of 'facts' could be separated from 'values'. Children spend 20 per cent of their time in school, so the importance of a school's role is obvious. Historically, universities and schools recognized their role in preparing men and women for their private and public lives. However, one of the casualties of the pell-mell rush towards a more individualistic approach has been civic responsibility. 'Looking out for number one' has a poisonous effect as individualism encourages people to opt out and to privatize their lives – becoming limited by the narrow confines of their job or their home. Only in Britain would we turn 'community service' into a punishment dispensed by magistrates. Citizenship has also been a casualty of the sheer complexity and overpowering nature of modern life. So often this has incapacitated citizens. We have come a long way from Athens, and on the road we have been robbed of our inheritance. Ill-prepared for the ethical and moral dilemmas, robbed of the concepts of duty and service, utility and functionalism have turned us into slaves of everything from a genetically manipulated reproductive system to the servility of consumerism. We are less like citizens and more like slaves.

The educators have become what C.S. Lewis in *The Abolition of Man* memorably called 'the conditioners'.[7] These 'conditioners' have made 'men without chests' from whom we expect

---

[7] C.S. Lewis, *The Abolition of Man* (Oxford: Oxford University Press, 1944).

'virtue and enterprise'. Lewis concluded that through modern formation 'we castrate and then bid the geldings to be fruitful'.[8] Aristotle urged that we educate for virtue, for duty, and for the common life. The conditioners say that it is all a matter of individual opinion, that individuals are not responsible for their actions. What have been the consequences? What is the dowry the conditioners can hand to their daughters? What is the legacy for the men without chests?

In the nineteenth century Carlyle called it 'the condition of England' question. In what condition do we find our country today? How a nation treats its children is a pretty good test of its claims to be civilized. It also sets in a proper context the scale of the challenge in forming tomorrow's citizens.

Eight hundred thousand British children now have no contact with their fathers; since 1961 marriage breakdown has increased by 600 per cent, with the number of divorces doubling since 1971. Many children have no experience of family life and no model on which to build loving and caring relationships.

Children are daily robbed of their innocence. Computer pornography, much involving children, and paedophile rings, many operating with the connivance of people in authority at children's homes and in social services or special hospitals, compete with the daily fare of advertising targeted at children. Never-ending computer games, films and TV programmes saturated with violence complement the pimps and drug pushers who operate like urban cadres on our streets, recruiting children and young people at every opportunity.

Broadcasters have colossal power in forming citizens – who spend an average of 27 hours a week in front of their TV sets. In a lecture to the television industry Bruce Gyngell, Managing Director of Tyne Tees Television, asked, 'What are we doing to our sensibilities and moral values and, more important, those of our children, when, day after day, we broadcast an unremitting

[8] Ibid.

diet of violence … television is in danger of becoming a mire of salaciousness and violence.' By contrast, in an interview in the UK press, Oliver Stone, who made the film *Natural Born Killers*, is quoted as saying, 'We poke fun at the idea of justice, at the idea of righteousness, at the concept that there is a right and a wrong way.' These sentiments should be a central concern for all who care about the formation of citizens.

In his book *Britain on the Couch*, the psychologist Oliver James asks the question, 'Why are we unhappier than we were in the 1950s despite being richer?'[9] Clinical depression, he says, is 10 times higher among people born after 1945 than among those born before 1914. Women under the age of 35 are the most vulnerable. The paradox is that we are told that we have never been more materially affluent and yet, says James, modern life seems less and less able to meet our expectations. We feel like losers, even if we are winners.

According to Gallup, in a survey of comparative attitudes in 1997 and 1968: in 1968, 62 per cent thought behaviour was getting worse; today it is 92 per cent. In 1968, 28 per cent thought they were happier; today the figure is 7 per cent, with 53 per cent believing that life is becoming unhappier. Only one per cent believed that standards of honesty in contemporary Britain were improving.

Consumerism, material gain, the high-tech, high-powered, information-laden lives of the 1990s are mirrored by collapsed family life, broken communities, the instability and insecurity in employment which accompanies market forces, and a widespread sense of isolation, from which flows loneliness. Like the disappointed ancient Greeks who finally climbed Olympus to search out their gods, modern men and women have scaled the peaks of prosperity and found nothing. They realize that instead of truth, they have been peddled a gigantic lie. When they ask for bread, we fill them with broken glass.

[9] O. James, *Britain on the Couch* (London: Century, 1997).

So many of our modern contemporaries find a void on the mountain top and resort to the escapism of the drugs scene, the couches of shrinks, the embrace of astrologers and the clutches of the black arts. This modern loneliness, which breeds despair, is fed by a diet of nihilism and materialism initiated from outside the home or the community. One German study states that between the ages of 3 and 13, a child watches an average of 107 minutes of TV each day. The German child psychologist Mrs Christa Meves found that 44 per cent of pre-school children preferred watching their TV to being with their father. Forty-nine per cent of videos bought or rented in Germany contain violent material.[10]

The poison is often in the dosage and this will intensify with digital TV – the ultimate amalgamation of the internet and TV, the proliferation of video material and games, the ethical and conceptual dilemmas posed by the use of virtual reality and subliminal techniques: these are the new environment for Britons, and everybody else, on the couch.

Virtue must be promoted; vice can make it on its own. Instead of virtuous citizens, we have been forming couch potatoes rather than discerning men and women with civilized and civilizing attitudes. We have learnt everything except the ability to become fully human. We are no longer Romans, but we are nothing else either. Who is to blame?

Parents blame teachers and vice versa; both blame the State. The politicians blame the broadcasters. Fear induces panic and, while latter-day Luddites would happily smash the internet and the TV sets, or string up newspaper editors, liberals are fright-ened to concede that anything at all is wrong, fearful that an honest admission would bring down their whole edifice.

Rosalind Miles, in *The Children We Deserve*, eloquently sums up the problem:

---

[10] C. Meves, speaking to a conference in Vienna in September 1997.

Part of the experience of growing up is learning to negotiate and to have social skills that come from relating to other people. If a child comes home from school, raids the fridge, and disappears to their room to the TV or computer console, that child is alienated. He or she will become cut off from real life and will come to expect instant gratification attuned to their needs. This is the foundation of yobbishness and violence.[11]

Academics, as ever, agonize over the empirical evidence. The evidence of our own eyes should be quite enough. However, there are studies which reveal that TV can trigger suppressed fears in children, or neurosis; that the lowest school achievers watch most TV, while the highest achievers watch the least. Some studies suggest that not only can obsessive TV-watching lead to retardation in language and mental performance, but it is blatantly obvious that programmes promote anti-parent feelings or ridicule institutions, as well as triggering solitude and an inability to integrate. In day-to-day conversation people talk endlessly about TV figures and characters – not about reality.

The internet may permit me to kiss my wife goodnight from New York or Paris, but it is not and never can be real. The danger is that we simply escape from reality. In the *Pensées*, Pascal says we are always trying to flee reality to near-real worlds – for example, a love of the past can become an attempt to escape the harsh challenges of today. Modern media have encompassed a new ideology of virtual reality.

Truth is a casualty as simple slogans, repeated *ad nauseam* in the media, become true. Why should we care about reality when the virtual will suffice? In addition to nihilism, reflected in political negative campaigning, spin-doctors ensure that the image and virtual-reality politics count more than substance or truth.

In our homes, the ideology of virtual reality allows us, through computer software, to kill, maim, brutalize or abuse another,

[11] R. Miles, *The Children We Deserve* (London: HarperCollins, 1994).

without any apparent consequences. We start to feel like gods, creators of the world with all of life's chances at our fingertips. God and creation become nothing but human invention. For some this is confirmation of Nietzsche's philosophy that man creates the universe, and it is a new extension of the serpent's promise in the Garden. In the Middle Ages, Thomas à Kempis well understood this impulse when he wrote in the *Imitation of Christ* that 'because men wanted to become God, God wanted to become man'[12] – to sanctify and redeem us from this conceit.

In response to corrosive external influences, families are patronizingly told to get a grip and use the off button. Yet vast numbers of households no longer house families where there are parents to perform this task; others house tired, pressurized, stressed parents who use the TV to replace the hearth or the baby-sitter and simply fail to discern between different categories of programmes. One 16-year-old girl told me, 'I live as a stranger in my own family.'

The destruction of family life leads inexorably to a dysfunctional society. Melanie Phillips in *All Must Have Prizes* perceptively analyses the consequences of this collapse.[13] In the American context, Allan Bloom in *The Closing of the American Mind* spells out the implications for citizenship when personal commitments and bonds can be broken or sloughed off, when the concept of fault is abolished, and when children's interests are reduced to the deceit that they would be somehow better off: 'Of course many families are unhappy. But that is irrelevant. The important lesson that the family teaches is the existence of the only unbreakable bond, for better or for worse, between human beings.'[14]

It is within the family – the basic building block of society – that a love of civic life must first be cultivated. Young women, like the 16-year-old girl I mentioned, must not be strangers to

---

[12] T. à Kempis, *The Imitation of Christ* – a new reading of the 1441 Latin autograph manuscript by William C. Creasy (Macon, Ga: Mercer University Press, 1989).
[13] M. Phillips, *All Must Have Prizes* (London: Little, Brown & Co., 1996).
[14] A. Bloom, *The Closing of the American Mind* (New York: Simon & Schuster, 1987).

their parents, or in their own homes. Ironically, those TV-resistant families who do shield their children may breed emotionally more stable and more mature children, but we will see another elite emerge: children unscathed by the ravages of uninhibited exposure to the electronic media.

There is plenty we can do, in the three areas of technology, the law and education, to support the family, but political will would be required. These should be central questions for the politicians and media. They are certainly central questions about the formation of citizens. The Archbishop of Canterbury, George Carey, perceived this when he said in a House of Lords debate in 1996 that the nation was being threatened by a tendency 'to view what is good and right as a matter of private taste and individual opinion only'.

With what sort of values have the conditioners, the men without chests, left us? They have replaced the Beatitudes with the Me-attitudes, and with individualism, relativism, syncretism, libertarianism and false liberalism. In fashioning a 'who-can-I-blame?', 'who-can-I-sue?', 'what-does-it-matter?', 'why-should-I-care?' society, they have left us poor beyond belief.

The human ecology is in tatters. Consider again our children. In 1996, 46,000 children were on child protection registers; 64,000 children were in local authority care; while a recent ICM poll found that 28 per cent of British parents thought their children were running wild. Crime is largely committed by young people – with 50 per cent of all crimes committed by those under 21. Ten times as many crimes are committed as in 1955 and the crime rate is 40 times that of 1901. In the United States, a baby born in 1990 and raised in a big city has a statistically greater chance of being murdered than an American soldier had of dying in battle in the Second World War. What goes into the formation of these young people is far more important than the debate about curfews and custodial sentences.

In Britain hardly a family or community is untouched by crime, violence or drugs. More than 160 babies were born addicted to purified cocaine during one 12-month period alone, and a recent study by the University of Manchester found that in the Northwest, 71 per cent of the region's adolescents had been offered drugs over a 12-month period.

Before we are born we are more likely than ever to be violently done away with. Only four out of every five pregnancies now goes full term. Six hundred babies are aborted daily. Since 1990, if you have a disability you may be aborted up to and even during your birth. One hundred thousand human embryos are now destroyed annually in British laboratories. Euthanasia and eugenics are regularly practised – not just in Holland and Scandinavia – and the old mistakes, which have led to episodes of genocide, racial theories and corrupt medical ethics, are dressed up in the new guise of genetics.

Everything is reduced to a matter of personal choice. The word itself originates from the same Greek word as the word 'heresy'. My right to choose – and never mind the consequences – is the modern heresy. Human life is reduced to a commodity: bought or bartered, experimented upon, tampered with, destroyed or disposed of at will. 'If it's right for me, it's right *per se*.'

In *The City of History* Lewis Mumford perceptively and prophetically saw how the balance of civil society was threatened:

> Before modern man can gain control over the forces that now threaten his very existence, he must resume possession of himself. This sets the chief mission for the city of the future: that of creating a visible regional and civic structure, designed to make man at home with his deeper self and his larger world, attached to images of human nature and love.[15]

Mumford foresaw the need to address the question of human development and personal expression. He appreciated the scale of de-industrialization which would occur, the social problems

---

[15] L. Mumford, *The City of History* (Harmondsworth: Pelican, 1961).

which would flow from this and the need to invest heavily in education: 'Not industry, but education will be the centre of their [cities'] activities.'

In practice, over the 35 years which have elapsed since Mumford argued for the centrality of the personal formation of citizens, economic and industrial regeneration have taken priority. Failure to appreciate the role of education in fostering a civilized society, where personal civic responsibility is cultivated in each person, has threatened the delicate balance which enables society to function. Among the consequences have been:

- the increasing isolation of the individual within the context of the modern urban environment;
- the fracturing of community bonds and their corresponding effects on the relationship of individuals to the State;
- the low levels of participation in the institutions and processes of local and national government;
- the lack of understanding about civic responsibilities and duties in the democratic State;
- the lack of a co-ordinated approach towards corporate responsibility and involvement in the community;
- the failure of citizens to understand what responsible citizenship in modern society really means.

Civil society has become uncivil as modern citizenship has become perceived in terms of rights alone. This in turn breeds unrealizable demands and a cult of selfishness which is bound to flourish in a climate of materialism and consumerism. It is further entrenched in the isolation of individualism and the marginalization of ethics. Is it any wonder that society becomes chronically disordered?

Rights and choice are the new civic dogma. Rights have replaced duties as propagandists demand the right to a job, the right to an education, the right to a child, the right to drugs, the right to pornography, the right to kill, the right to die. Displaced are the ancient duties to work, to acquire knowledge, to care for the family, to cherish and to respect life. Choices are no longer conditioned by consequences. The delicate balance of civil society is thus broken. In his justly famous book *After Virtue*, Alasdair MacIntyre poses the central question of whether new communal and civic relationships can be snatched from the poisonous clutches of individualism.[16]

This is the second area which I want to explore: the political and educational response. Failure to address at any level of the curriculum the role of citizens and the question of citizenship in modern society, the absence of a coherent approach in industry in cultivating corporate responsibility or civic engagement, and the general lack of understanding about what are a citizen's duties and responsibilities in a democratic state, are the key questions for the twenty-first century. Failure to address them properly will lead to further civic disengagement and dysfunction.

If we were to educate for citizenship and take seriously the civic deficit, we would enshrine the duties of each person: to live peaceably; to participate in civic government; to contribute to the resourcing of commonly beneficial institutions; to acquire knowledge and encourage the pursuit of knowledge in children; to learn respect for the needs of others; to behave ethically; to appreciate how legitimate rights have been acquired and to cherish them. We need a greater concern with how civil society is made, how it decays and how it might be preserved. Civic education is a *sine qua non*.

If a civil society is to withstand the ambitions of those who wish to usurp it, fundamental shared principles must be widely held and understood in the political community and beyond. A nation or community will not survive for long if its civil structures are corrupted or decaying, or if its rulers and citizens do not pursue civic virtues. A respect for the sanctity of human life, respect for law, a sense of personal responsibility, public spirit

[16] A. MacIntyre, *After Virtue* (London: Duckworth, 1981).

and munificence, firmness of purpose, discernment and fore-
sight, perseverance and a sense of duty might be chief among
these civic qualities. Aristotle celebrated justice, wisdom,
temperance and courage as the cardinal virtues and associated
with these were magnanimity, liberality, munificence, prudence
and gentleness. Christ offered the virtues of faith, hope and
charity – the love of God in its original meaning. If such indispensable virtues are not passed from generation to generation,
civic fabric is bound to crumble.

These are not new concerns. In *Politics* Aristotle's notion of
civic virtue was exemplified by a concern for the rights of others,
in the civilizing of the *polis* and through a sense of justice. Aristotle said we are not like 'solitary pieces in chequers', but need to
cultivate a common life.[17] Cicero, in his work 'On Duty', also saw
the need for active participation: 'The whole glory of virtue is in
activity.'[18] Aristotle believed that civic virtue could and should be
taught.

Aristotle also held that there was something innate about a
citizen's desire to participate in the public life. *Zoon politikon*,
political animal, is a phrase which he coined in his *Politics* and
which remains in regular, contemporary usage. Today it has
perjorative connotations, but for Aristotle it was an honourable
phrase denoting a citizen who strove for others. For Aristotle,
communal existence – *koinonia* – was not about civic structures
or forms of government, but primarily about the qualities in man
which made civic coexistence a possibility. Man alone, he
argued, had the *logos*, the ability to speak, but more than that,
man had the ability to use reason and to act as a moral agent.
'Man alone has the special distinction from the other animals
that he also has perception of good and bad and of the just and
the unjust.'

---

[17] Aristotle, *Politics*, Books 1–2, translated with a commentary by Trevor J.
     Saunders (Oxford: Clarendon, 1995).
[18] Cicero, 'On Duty', in *Speeches* (London: Heinemann, 1931).

Aristotle described the *polis* as 'an association of free men' which governed itself; where the citizen 'takes turn to govern and be governed', familiar territory for the modern democrat always expectant of losing or winning public office. The *polis* became the school of life. The *polis*, through its laws, religion, traditions, festivals, culture and participation in its common institutions, shaped each citizen. Its architecture, its theatre (the nearest equivalent in Athenian society to our concept of a free press, particularly plays which dared to satirize and to explore controversial questions), its orators, its laws – all were manifestations of the common life and all required the commitment of the citizens. It was a duty to engage in the *polis*, sharing in the glories as well as the burdens. A man who withdrew from the life of the *polis* was not perceived as simply minding his own business, living a private life, but as being a worthless good-for-nothing. The city's business was everyone's business and participation in the life of the city was crucial to a person's development. Taking part was not an optional extra.

Rewards and punishments help to mould a man's attributes and Aristotle held that a man would endure danger because of a combination of civic commitment to the common good and a fear of the shame and legal penalties, the punishments, which would attach to cowardice or civic indolence. *Aidos* – fear of shame, of how you would appear to other citizens – is for Aristotle the balancing scale in the civic question. It balances the cherished ideal that the citizen would want to act nobly and altruistically.

Closer to our own times, Gertrude Himmelfarb, in her book *The De-moralisation of Society: From Victorian Virtues to Modern Values*,[19] reminds us that the Victorians also focused on good character and personal responsibility. They spoke not so much about values but of virtues – a more demanding test. No doubt

[19] G. Himmelfarb, *The De-moralisation of Society: From Victorian Virtues to Modern Values* (Institute of Economic Affairs, Health & Welfare Unit, 1995).

there was an element of romanticism implicit in the Victorian emphasis, calling up medieval codes of courtly chivalry – the virtues of mercy, religion, compassion and courtesy. But the caricature of Victorian virtue as largely hypocritical and enforced by Dickensian schoolmasters is just that: a caricature. The Victorian pursuit of virtue was as much about encouragement as it was about imposition. It was primarily aimed at creating a civic community of citizens who respected one another and were determined to advance and improve themselves. Perhaps it is best revealed in the civic municipalism of Chamberlain's Birmingham.

It is a pity that the word 'values' has become interchangeable with the word 'virtues'. Leo Strauss was right to muse on the mystery of 'how a word which used to mean the manliness of man has come to mean the chastity of women'.[20] Friedrich Nietzsche was, in the 1880s, the first to stop talking about virtue and to use values in the modern sense of describing collective attitudes and beliefs. 'Transvaluation of values', as he put it, disposed of virtue and vice, classical virtues, Judaeo-Christian virtues, good and evil, and conveniently accompanied 'the death of God'.[21]

Alongside virtue, 'value' is a weak word. It can mean anything people want it to mean, which is why it works so well against a backdrop of syncretism and relativism. Everything becomes neutral and nonjudgemental; nothing is absolutely right or absolutely wrong. A return to the concept of civic virtue would prove to be the best defence against civic disaggregation and provide the basis for a new civic settlement – a settlement about more than a devolved Scottish Parliament or reformed House of Lords.

'Virtue' is a word which is not simply about personal preference or personal views. It is about character and the formation

---

20 Quoted by Himmelfarb, ibid.
21 See F. Nietzsche, *The Genealogy of Morals* (Harmondsworth: Penguin, 1997).

of the citizen at the deepest level. Civic life and politics are conditioned by the culture in which they grow. If the character of the citizen has not been fully formed, and is deficient in virtue, is it any wonder that social anarchy results? Can we avoid this? Can civic virtue be taught? Can we educate for citizenship?

Since the virtual disappearance of civics courses, even that narrow preparation for citizenship has not been a priority in schools. The many other pressures of the national curriculum mean that provision is patchy at best and nonexistent at worst. One survey suggests that nearly a third of primary schools are not addressing the themes of citizenship, while Leicester University's Centre for Citizenship Studies has published valuable data – including a plea by almost half the primary schools for more staff training and access to resource material and visiting speakers.

The last thing which teachers or pupils need is another subject for examination. That is not what the White Paper and any subsequent legislation or curriculum requirements should seek to achieve. We need a sustained, rigorous and properly resourced approach to a subject which cuts to the heart of how a society functions. This should replace the 'mission statements' of many educational institutions which simply contain lip-service reference to citizenship. The reality is that most pupils, students, administrators, teachers and faculty members could not tell you how that objective relates to either the curriculum or to the day-to-day policy of the institution.

When we recognize academic achievements and sporting prowess, we should also recognize instances of good citizenship. In many American universities credits are given for community work. We need to practise and experience citizenship as well as analyse it. Service learning, where those with advantages teach literacy to the disadvantaged, especially commends itself to me. At school prize-giving and degree day ceremonies, citizenship awards should be presented and be a formal part of individual records of achievement.

For most young people civic education is generally acquired as an incidental, through contacts with voluntary projects and with individual teachers, or because of an event or political policy which directly impinges upon them. We must be far more systematic and, in courses at every level, ask the tough questions about the purpose of education, about what is expected of democratic citizens, about our culture and the values which pervade it, and about the skills we each require to live peaceably. It is part of the mission of a school or university to educate for democracy, to develop citizenship skills and to form men and women for others.

How a citizen acts as a moral agent affects everything from how they treat their environment and their neighbours to the pursuit of ethical standards in commerce or the embrace of civic duties. It is not a spectator sport or the preserve of a few well-meaning specialists.

Before the collapse of the Soviet Union many of us saw first-hand the consequences of the destruction of civil society. Loss of freedom is all too obvious when you have been run over by a tank. The corrosive effect of materialism and individualism is less obvious. Here the devil arrives in carpet slippers. Early twentieth-century Marxist obsession with production, the division of labour and class structures has been matched by individualistic indifferentism in our own times. The disfigurement of civic culture and the suppression of civil order have been the principal casualties. At its worst, atrocious power has come to be exercised by a rump over the rest of the human race.

If we are to avoid such disaster, each of us must understand our duty to our country and to the community. The complete citizen will be a virtuous citizen: one who has been formed to consider and care for others. We will each still have our individual frailties, weaknesses and vices, but even from the worst of us some good can be extracted. In his *Fable of the Bees* – or 'Private Vices, Publick Benefits' – Bernard Mandeville recognized how this might happen:

Thus every part was full of Vice
Yet the whole mass a Paradise…
And Vertue, who from Politicks
Had learn'd a Thousand cunning Tricks;
Was, by their happy influence,
Made Friends with Vice: And ever since
The worst of all the Multitude
Did something for the Common Good.[22]

[22] B. Mandeville, *Fable of the Bees*, edited with an introduction by Phillip Harth (Harmondsworth: Penguin, 1970).

CITIZENSHIP: NOT AN ACADEMIC QUESTION

David Blunkett

8 MARCH 1999

The Rt Hon. David Blunkett MP is the Secretary of State for Education and Employment and the Labour Member of Parliament for Sheffield. He was formerly the Leader of Sheffield Council.

Liverpool is a warm and vibrant place, and with that vibrancy comes a sense of community, of civic pride – a belief in the commitment to community which is so easily lost, but which is rarely engaged these days in terms of formalized democratic procedures. That is why it is so important to re-engage the debate about what we mean by citizenship, what it means for us and those around us, and how we can relate the formal and the informal together.

A recent article in the *Sunday Times* sought to have a go at the whole concept of teaching citizenship, and at me for actually daring, as Secretary of State, to want citizenship to be part of the curriculum. Anyone, everyone, should have a say in this, apparently, except myself. Well, I can celebrate a lifetime of commitment to citizenship – 25 years as a trustee of Community Service Volunteers, a member of the Speaker's Commission on Citizenship under the former Speaker of the House of Commons, someone who is not a Johnny-come-lately to citizenship, but, like David Alton, has had a deep, lifelong commitment to ensuring that we engage with each other and do not just preach political slogans at each other.

There are some very funny little stories which bring alive the importance of understanding what is going on around us in our politics and our citizenship. I met a nursery head the other day who told me that, while she was buttoning up the little dufflecoat of a four-year-old, she took the risk of asking him who he thought the Prime Minister was. Without hesitation, and with the kind of adenoidal response you get in both South Yorkshire and Liverpool, he said, 'Toby Bear'. Well, he nearly got it right – and the Prime Minister was good enough to laugh when I told him about it.

It is important that we understand the formalities of what is happening around us, but it is also important that we engage with it in all sorts of different ways. There was a time, many moons ago, when I thought that the only true engagement was shown by people who were prepared to turn up to tedious meetings week after week in smoke-filled rooms. When I first joined the Labour Party, there was water coming through the roof (incidentally, that made me decide that teachers should not have to teach with water coming through the roof), in circumstances that were inclined to turn you off politics and active citizenship rather than turn you on. I now believe very strongly in engagement in formal politics, in people playing a part in their civic community, but I also understand very well that, for the majority of citizens, it will be their active engagement *with each other* which displays their commitment and caring, their active citizenship in their own lives. It is about building from the foundations which all of us cherish, understanding that we are so much more when we work together as part of a strong community, supporting and enabling individuals to develop their talents.

There is a very old saying that was brought alive a year or two ago by Hillary Clinton: 'It takes a village to educate a child.' Of course, without education the village itself is unlikely to be alive, vibrant and able to cope, and that is as true of a large city as it is of a village. The foundation on which we build is the family. The world that is constructed to make that foundation safe is the community, and the cement which holds it together is education

– education not simply in terms of instilling the basics (crucial though that is), but education for the whole person. There is no conflict between teaching children to read, write and do maths to an acceptable level and taking a holistic approach to teaching them about the world around, providing them with the commitment that will ensure a civilized and acceptable society. There is no division between engaging children in creativity and encouraging a love of the arts and culture, and teaching them to share their talent and their imagination with others. In other words, the ladder of enlightenment is as important as the ladder of lifelong learning. The two must go hand in hand if we are to succeed as a society in the new century.

Of course, now we also need to modernize, to engage with the world of information and communication technology. Above all, we must avoid creating a new gap between the haves and the have-nots in a knowledge-based, information age, where understanding how to use and when not to use computers, being computer literate and being able to draw down information from the web will all be seen as crucial life skills. You cannot do it without basic education in terms of the ability to operate the equipment, but, even more, you cannot do it without the ability to read and write.

In this context, I must pay tribute to people such as Phil Redmond from Merseyside, who has helped us with the development of the National Year of Reading and with a commitment to adult literacy through the 'Brookie Basics' programme. It is a tremendous contribution towards enabling people to take up their citizenship in full, to engage in full for themselves and their family and for the community around them. For the family, for a successful community, for the development and worth of education, we need to put those elements together. Having a job, having some sense of security in an ever-changing and insecure world, helps to avoid the disintegration and fracturing of our society. We need to make education and citizenship work hand in hand.

Seventy-five per cent of those on remand in Britain have a reading age of 10 or less. There are two conclusions we can draw from this. One is that we have the most ignorant and illiterate criminals in the world. The other is that illiteracy and lack of education, lack of self-belief, self-expectation and self-reliance, go hand in hand with criminal activity and alienation from our society. We know the latter is true. We know also that generational disadvantage is passed on in a way that accelerates the downward trend.

I read in the *Daily Mail* recently of a family on Reservoir Street in Liverpool. It was not one of the archetypal *Daily Mail* articles. It was not intending to expose or have a go at anything. It simply described a family where no one worked, where older sisters and brothers of the one youngster who was still at school had disengaged from education, and where there was a lack of expectation that the youngster himself would have the opportunity of success. These factors transformed the life chances of every single one of them, and severely reduced the school's chances of being able to do the job. In order to overcome the cynicism that undermines, erodes and corrodes our society, it is crucial that we engage with each other, actively support families in their development, and bring alive the belief that it is possible for every youngster – from whatever background – to be able to thrive and have a successful future.

If I could wish away one thing, it would be the cynics that erode every opportunity of changing the world. That is why the Foundation for Citizenship – an alliance that draws together a whole range of organizations in committing themselves to active citizenship – is so crucial. From the very moment children enter school, they should be able to believe in themselves, but also learn how to be committed to mutuality, interdependence and helping others.

An active, full and participatory life is an active, full citizenship contribution. We have to feel part of, have a stake in, be valued by the community in which we live and work. To make that possible, we have to value each other, we have to develop self-reliance – part of the glue of a community which knows that we can only succeed by doing it together. That is why the commitment to universal literacy, to shared goals, is so important. I read all the theory when I studied politics as a mature student at university – Rousseau, John Stuart Mill and adult educators such as R.H. Tawney and Harold Silver. A commitment to adult education was ingrained in me: through night school and day release, it took me six years to get to university. There I found that, at that time, less than 10 per cent of students made it to university. At that time you also found that the youngsters you met there were no brighter than the people you had left behind on the council estate – those who never imagined that they could actually make it and be able to succeed in that way.

Our task is to transform those expectations, but also to understand that it is not simply about succeeding in formal education. It is also about the change we can bring about in the morality of politics and social activity. I would love us to be able to debate, as we did at university, the morality of politics rather than the political lack of morality which engages the media today. We do not talk about political morality in terms of the policies and values that we seek to implement or challenge. The only political morality that is debated in this country today is illustrated best by people's sexual proclivities or the borrowing of their friends' money. I am, of course, not against debating where we are and what we do as politicians, but it would be nice to debate where we are going as a society, so that through lifelong learning we can renew a commitment to something broader than the immediate and minor concerns that so often engage us.

That is why I set up the Committee under Professor Bernard Crick. The accusation that he is an old professor of mine is true: he is. He wrote all about citizenship and political literacy 30 years ago. In fact, he got so disgruntled with undergraduates, when I was an undergraduate at Sheffield University, that he left to become Head of Politics at Birkbeck, where he would meet mature, part-time students. Those were the revolutionary days there, I would say – not when students chanted at you about tuition fees, but when they refused to take examinations at all on the grounds that they crowded out the real educative things they wanted to do. I am an old codger when it comes to revolutionary politics.

Bernard Crick drew together a whole range of people, including those who take a very different view of politics from me, such as Kenneth Baker. He then carried a unanimous report about the way forward and the way in which we need to engage with learning outcomes – not with the dead hand of forcing a particular pattern on people, but with learning outcomes that ensure we have a commitment to citizenship. He talked about three key areas:

1 Social and moral responsibility: learning about rights and responsibilities, yes, but also about rules, authority, responsible decision-making and debate – the ability to settle our differences in an acceptable fashion.
2 Community involvement: becoming helpfully engaged in the life and concerns of the community, undertaking active citizenship, being part of the very lifeblood of the neighbourhood.
3 Political literacy: not party political literacy, but developing skills, knowledge and the attributes of an enquiring mind – being able to negotiate, to debate, to resolve competing interests without violence or thuggery, creating a society where the morality of the individual, the commitment to the community, the political literacy of being able to operate in that society, were able to come together.

It is my intention that we should take this forward. There is no question of squeezing out other subjects such as religious education or history. We are talking about a synergy, bringing subject areas together, engaging the different disciplines, being able to engage people's minds in looking at one society and one part of our history, looking at spirituality and what is important in people's lives, understanding world religions and what it means for us in our communities. We are talking about engaging with a future world where – God willing – we will never have the racist murder of Stephen Lawrence repeated, and where the unaccept-able murder of Philip Lawrence will evoke a commitment to renewing an understanding of decency and citizenship in our education service.

It seems to me that, if we are not to engage in angst and gesturism, it is crucial that we debate the aftermath of the Stephen Lawrence enquiry sanely. We do not want to go back to inventing anti-racist units in order to irritate people: we want real action for change that engages with people's minds and atti-tudes, and with the nature of the society in which they operate. Of course, employment will be crucial. Of course, education and the foundations that need to be laid in working with families at the earliest possible juncture will be critical. Of course, creating a society in which people *can* operate in an acceptable fashion will matter, but it will also be crucial that we engage young people at the earliest possible stage with an understanding of the world they live in and the treatment of others around them.

I learnt a long time ago about the importance of tolerance, but, in tackling racism, tolerance is not enough. Tolerance applies to those things which irritate us, which we dislike but, as civilized human beings, we are prepared to tolerate in each other – the mannerisms, the actions, that all of us have to learn to live with in each other because we are all full of them. That is not how we overcome racism. We do not want people simply to be tolerant of each other because of race or colour: we want them to under-stand that they do not have to talk of tolerance at all, because it simply would not occur to someone in a civilized society that they needed to do so because of the colour of someone's skin. It is as deep as that and as difficult as that. That is what we are trying to do in engaging with the broader programme of citizenship in our schools, colleges and society. We can do quite a lot by illustration.

The idea of mentoring is taking off. It could, and hopefully will, be seen as a trend: mentoring children in school; giving people the opportunity to see role models working in practice; engaging business and commerce in the idea so that people can be released from work to do it; citizenship programmes such as Millennium Volunteers, which we are developing with £45 million of government money. Mentoring can be undertaken by university students who are prepared to give their time and work in schools. It can be as simple as hearing a child read, or it can be as complicated as working with a young offender in difficult circumstances. Whatever form it takes, mentoring is a demonstration of active citizenship and it will enable us to make real progress, whether we are tackling racism and vandalism or disengagement and alienation.

Progress is already being made; there are changes occurring in our society. In reducing the divide, we are beginning to succeed by working together. Our schools are succeeding in terms of the equality of opportunity for different races. Take the following statistics, for example. This year, 47 per cent of white youngsters achieved five high-grade GCSEs. It was only 29 per cent of black youngsters, but it was only 23 per cent of them the year before. It was only 33 per cent of Bangladeshi youngsters, but it was only 25 per cent the year before. It was 53 per cent of Indian youngsters, but it was only 48 per cent the year before. It was 61 per cent of Chinese and Southeast Asian youngsters, the same figure as the year before, so they outstrip all of us.

Just as progress is being made in our schools, so there is a change taking place in our communities. We have a very long way to go, but there are now a million more families with someone in work than there were three years ago. There are 400,000 people who work compared with just under two years ago. We have halved youth unemployment. Of course we have an enormous challenge in the most disadvantaged areas, in Liverpool and in my home city and area of Sheffield and South Yorkshire – two of the most disadvantaged areas in the country, which are designated for Objective One status in the European Union's new grant-funding round.

If we are going to do it properly, however, it is not simply a top-down government programme which is needed. Good as the New Deal is – and I am responsible for it – it will not solve the problems of the world. It will help. It should start by rooting back into policies like Sure Start, which work with families from the moment a child is born. Engaging volunteers from the nonstatutory sector will make a difference, but on its own it is still a government programme and it will not change the world. What *will* change the world is for communities to develop their own capacity to cope. This is called 'capacity building' now. It used to be called 'community development' when I was a lad. 'Social entrepreneurship' used to be called 'community leadership'. It does not matter what we call it – it is about communities and individuals taking hold of their own lives, but being able to do so with the support of others.

I think this is a doctrine that encompasses all sorts and no sorts of political ideology. It can engage people who would argue with each other if they sat down in a pub or after church, but who, in committing themselves in the community, actually share a similar objective. That is why it is so crucial that we get it right. The holistic approach I described earlier is writ large in terms of what we do in our education system, both for children and adults. We can do it. It is already being done. It is bringing neighbourhoods alive, and what it needs is the active support of those of us who have resources, structures and influence (not power, but influence) at our disposal. As a lifelong committed person wanting to ensure that others can take control of their lives and have a future built on their own self-confidence, I have every intention of making it work.

Some people are frightened of these issues; some people believe that there is too great a lack of confidence in our democracy, a lack of strength in our community and a lack of ability in each of us as individuals to be able to take on that challenge; some people would like to allow only the elite to make decisions or engage in political debate; some people are frightened of the big issues of the day reaching those whom they believe are not capable of coping with them. All these people not only live in the world of a bygone era, but they also live in a dream world where they disengage the millions in order to ensure that their particular view of the world is not challenged. Well, I do not mind being challenged day in and day out, and I think that, if the challenge is taken up by people who have underpinned their ability to cope with differences by having already learnt how to solve problems sensibly, how to develop differences equally, how to treat each other fairly, then we will have a society that is worth living in.

REWORKING CITIZEN DUTIES

Jack Straw

12 APRIL 1999

The Rt Hon. Jack Straw MP is the Home Secretary and the Member of Parliament for Blackburn. He is a former president of the National Union of Students.

Two weeks ago I was invited to present the Lambeth Young Citizens' Awards in Brixton. These awards have been the idea of a local police officer who wanted to pay tribute to those in her area who have really made a difference to their community. Something that was very moving, as the citations for the awards were read out by this police officer, was that the young people receiving these awards were in no sense goody-two-shoes who had never been in trouble with their parents, the police or their schools. Most of them had a record of one kind or another, but, through a good deal of intervention and in some cases just through strength of character, they had become eligible for awards for real heroism, for endeavour and for contribution to the community.

Nineteen young people were given awards, but the one who received the premier award was a young woman aged 17 who had witnessed a very savage attack in her area and had decided to do something about it. She decided, in spite of all the intimidation she received, that she was going to report this to the police, that she was going to provide witness statements, and that she was going to go forward and give evidence – a real act of citizenship if ever there was one. She survived, and the area prospered.

As I was giving out the awards, I wondered what the concept of citizenship actually meant to those young people. How often did they talk about the idea of citizenship? The answer, I suspect, would be, 'Not very much.' Citizenship is not a term which we use very much in our daily lives. We may regard ourselves as Londoners or Liverpudlians, as fans of Everton, Tranmere Rovers or Blackburn, as students of life or of Liverpool John Moores University – but we very rarely identify ourselves as *citizens*. Indeed, citizenship has never been a term of very great emotional significance for the British, even though it was British thinkers like Tom Paine who did much to shape the way the world thinks about the rights of man and to develop the concepts of democracy and citizenship in the nineteenth century.

I think a big part of this absence of self-consciousness about citizenship may be because British society has never been through the sort of revolutionary upheaval which spawns bills of rights and new constitutions. France has gone through one monarchy, two empires and five republics, while Britain has stayed simply a parliamentary monarchy (although it has had its challenging moments, of course). The basic system of government here has evolved rather than been the subject of a convulsion. We are unique in that regard in Europe, and I cannot think of one country (with the possible exception of Andorra, Liechtenstein, San Marino and maybe Luxembourg), one major country, on the mainland of Europe which has not experienced the convulsion of civil war, dictatorship, occupation by foreign troops or changes to their boundaries in the last 200 years.

I do think a lot about what we should do to improve education about citizenship in our society. One of the tools I think teachers ought to use is simply a historical atlas – to show the unchanging boundaries of this kingdom, certainly within the mainland of Great Britain, over a period of nearly 1,000 years, and then to show the extraordinary changes which have taken place within the last two centuries on the mainland of Europe. It would help to give people an understanding of why it is that we sometimes have a different perspective from others in Europe. Just remember, there were hundreds of states in Germany right up until 1870. Italy was also not united until that year. Perhaps we should also remember some of the contributing factors which led, literally, to the Balkanization of the Balkans from which we are still suffering today.

For us, such upheaval has passed us by and there has been no overnight change from being a subject to being a citizen. We seem happy enough being both. Perhaps the relative tranquillity of these shores is the reason why we all seem to take the idea of citizenship so much for granted. We do not ignore altogether what goes with citizenship, but our greatest emotional attachment to this cause tends to be focused on what have been described by Marshall as 'social rights' – things like education, health care and pensions; practical benefits which have accumulated over time, rather than legal or constitutional freedoms for which revolutions have been fought.

We are now moving into a period when we are almost bound to become much more conscious (and self-conscious) of our explicit rights and responsibilities as citizens, and of the relationship between each of us as individuals and the State. A nation which was characterized in the last century by having no written constitution at all is going to end this decade with at least a half-written constitution. This is made up of the international treaties and conventions which we have incorporated or are about to incorporate into our own law, the treaties of the European Union which now take precedence – and have done since 1973 – over our own law, and the wholly separate European Convention of Human Rights which is going to be incorporated into our law. For Scotland and Wales, there are the statutes establishing their parliament and assembly and executives, which amount to their written constitutions for the very high degree of self-government which they will enjoy after 6 May this year.

A proper and developed sense of citizenship does need a clear statement of rights and responsibilities, and that is what we as a Government (with, I am pleased to say, backing from all the other major parties in Parliament at the third reading) have sought to provide by incorporating within United Kingdom law the European Convention of Human Rights. For the first time ever in a British statute (not just since 1689 – that Bill of Rights fulfilled a rather different purpose), we have a core statement of basic protections which can be upheld through our courts. I believe that this Act will change the relationship between the State and the citizen, and it should also start to redress the dilution of rights which has taken place under previous governments – of both parties, let me say – which tended to be far too centralizing.

There is bound to be some anxiety about whether the implementation of the Act (it has not yet been brought into force and certainly will not be before next year) will be disruptive of our court and criminal justice processes. One of the reasons why we are taking our time before it is brought fully into law is to provide for proper training of judges, magistrates and everybody else involved in the criminal and justice systems, precisely so that it is not gratuitously disruptive.

The thing to remember about the European Convention of Human Rights is that, although it is called a European Convention and therefore some might say it is from 'that lot across the Channel', in fact the Convention states what British jurists saw as a considered statement of the rights and responsibilities of citizens in this country. They put those ideas together – the basic rights which we took for granted in this country, the rights of common law – and sought to loan them out for the benefit of people in Europe. Indeed, it was British jurists like David Maxwell Fife, who later became Lord Chancellor in the 1950s, who were the principal draughtsmen of the European Convention. It is paradoxical that, although British jurists literally laid down the law in the Convention, and although Britain played a leading role in the Council of Europe (the body which drew up and formally agreed the Convention), we are the last country in Europe to be incorporating it into our law.

Alongside the incorporation of the Convention and, indeed, the EU treaties, the people of Scotland and Wales and Northern Ireland respectively, Parliament and Assembly and executive bodies, whose constitution, powers and relationship to Westminster are not defined by convention as those of the Westminster Parliament are, nor by some recollection of pre-1689 prerogative rights, but are defined by a single text by their establishing statutes.

This, then, is the first reason why we have to become more assertive, more explicit, about the idea of citizenship in the United Kingdom. In our modern, evolving and increasingly written democracy, developing the idea of citizenship will help us better define the relationship between the individual and the State.

There are two other reasons, I would suggest, for becoming more assertive and explicit about the idea of citizenship. The first of these could be dismissed as a semantic point, but words have very great power, particularly for those of us who have to address the public and their needs. I am often, literally, lost for words about the proper term of address to use to an audience. For politicians in the United States, the answer is an easy, straightforward and inclusive one: the audience is the 'American people' or 'American citizens'. General de Gaulle used a different but equally inclusive form in those great broadcasts he used to make to the French people: he would begin his addresses to the nation with 'Français, Françaises'. In Britain, however, we get stuck if we're not careful and resort to the awkward, very condescending and exclusionary term 'ordinary people'. We do not know what to call other people, and this term normally implies that the speaker, but not his or her audience, is anything but ordinary. It automatically sets up a barrier between the person speaking and those who are listening. I think it is time to strike out 'ordinary people' from the political lexicon and to start talking about 'citizens' instead.

My other reason for saying that we need to be more explicit about the idea of citizenship leads on from the first two. Once the broad concept of citizenship is established in citizens' minds, it becomes much easier to develop the idea of citizenship in an active sense – i.e. how people can give something back to the community by voluntary activity and end up receiving much more than they have given. When I talk about the need to develop a more active definition of citizenship, I am not just talking about concepts derived from nationality law. The rights and responsibilities which individuals in this country enjoy are, for the most part, not confined to British citizens within the strict meaning of the word, nor should they be. The principle that the protection of the law should be extended to everyone, irrespective of their race, their culture or their nationality, is not some modern innovation. After all, slavery was declared unlawful within this country not because of any intrinsic rights which came from citizenship, but because of a sense of the rights which all people enjoyed simply through being here, rights which were developed from a sense of a basic or natural law. As a judge put it at the time, 'The air of England is too pure for a slave to have to breathe in.'

I am very conscious of the importance of all this through my role as Home Secretary. The office has a unique role in the development of the concept of citizenship. As Home Secretary, I am responsible for some of the oldest, perhaps most fundamental, identifiers of citizenship. These include access to justice and the right to the protection of the law; decisions as to who can or cannot enter the country, and who can or cannot claim British nationality; responsibility for the electoral process (although I am not responsible for the *outcome* of the electoral process, of course), including who can vote and how we vote. In a direct sense, therefore, thousands of Home Office staff, and ultimately myself as the elected Government Minister, have the power to decide on a day-to-day basis who can and who cannot be a citizen. It is a responsibility which we must never take lightly. In a mature democracy such as ours, those who make decisions on fundamental rights of citizenship have to expect intense public scrutiny. This, by the way, is a further reason why we are committed to introducing freedom of information legislation, to give every citizen the right of access to information held by public bodies.

Citizenship, as I have indicated, is not just about legal rights and legal enforcement. It should also have a positive, proactive side. I think citizenship is something worth celebrating, and worth celebrating in a conscious way. Compared with other countries, however, we have not been very good about this. Canada, Australia, the United States and many other countries honour new citizens on their respective national days, and other appropriate days, with public ceremonies and citations. What do we do in Britain for the people who become new citizens, who have said to all of us, as British citizens, that they wish to share in the fruits of the citizenship which we enjoy? What do we do? We send them a brown paper envelope through the post with a certificate, normally about two years late, such is the queue and the delay in processing applications.

Jonathan Friedland summed this up rather neatly in his book *Bringing Home the Revolution*. He said, 'While the Americans organize a tear-jerking ceremony for new citizens, the British authorities offer nothing. New Britons do not come together in a branch of the Home Office [they should be pleased about that!], but neither do they sing their national anthem and hear a warm speech of welcome. They do not weep in the embrace of relatives and their new country.' Although that may go too far for what is an old country (after all, Canada, Australia and the United States are all 'new' countries), I think that Mr Friedland has a point. We should be doing more to celebrate citizenship, to value those who take on the rights and responsibilities of citizenship by naturalization and acquisition as well as by birth. I would like to see us developing ways in which we can, literally, celebrate citizenship, ways in which citizenship certificates could be awarded in a proper ceremony to mark such a key rite of passage.

Being a citizen involves much more than having a piece of paper, of course. The right to vote is an area where eligibility and nationality are linked – though even here, interestingly, because this is Britain, there is no neat correlation. For many years, we have rightly allowed citizens of the Commonwealth and the Irish Republic who are resident here to vote in all of our elections. In more recent times, we have extended the franchise for European and local elections by allowing residents who are nationals from elsewhere in the European Union to take part. Despite this, however, we have poor turnout rates in elections, especially for local and European elections. Liverpool is something of a paradox in this sense. There is a great sense of citizenship in the city, a great sense of community involvement and community responsibility, and some very vibrant, not to say rough and tough, politics – but Liverpool wins the wooden spoon when it comes to participation in formal elections. I think we managed to get 12 per cent of the populace out for a European election, and there was also a local election where the poll dropped to just 6 per cent. This is not impressive. I am not just having a go at Liverpool. In Islington, where I was a councillor, it was 16 per cent, and in the central areas of Blackburn turnout has not been good either.

Perhaps it is one of the defining characteristics of being British that, having fought so hard over so many years for the core rights of citizenship such as the franchise, we should then be lackadaisical about taking advantage of them. This is something I would like to change, although not by going down the Australian route of compulsory voting. I fancy the police have better things to do than arrest people who have not voted. In any case, I take the view that, if people have a right to vote, they also have a right not to vote. When they do not vote, they may be saying something not only about themselves but also about the political process and their relation to it. I am not, therefore, suggesting compulsory voting. I do suggest, however, that we have to encourage much greater voting participation in a number of other ways.

We need to do that by introducing new ways of voting, ways which we hope will increase local democracy and accountability, and we have done that. We have the new system of European parliamentary elections, the regional list, coming up on 10 June. We have different systems in Scotland and Wales which will hopefully generate renewed interest in voting systems. When we elect a Mayor for London's Assembly next year, that will be a different system again – and if Liverpool wants a mayor and an assembly too, then there would be a different system for that. All of this may encourage people to play a greater part in the political process.

We also have to ensure that our electoral procedures are up to date and that they facilitate rather than hinder the electoral process. That is why I have established a working party on electoral procedures under the chairmanship of the Home Office Minister, good friend and Merseyside MP, George Howarth. This working party is currently considering all the procedural aspects of holding elections, including such issues as electronic voting, rolling registers, improvements in postal voting and absent voting, and the best day on which to hold an election. There are people who say we should hold elections on Saturdays and Sundays. I think there is a lot to be said for that, provided that we do not do what the Labour Party did last Saturday and hold a major rally (to which they invited me) on the same day as the Grand National. So there are some advantages in having the election on a Thursday, if you pick the right day, but there are also advantages in having it at a weekend. With overall turnout levels of only 35 per cent for European elections and less than 30 per cent for local elections outside London, there is an enormous need for greater encouragement of people to vote. To do that, we should not just be improving the process, we should also be developing the idea of good citizenship.

The former Speaker of the House of Commons, Lord Weatherill, in the introduction to a report of the Commission on Citizenship which he established in the late 1980s, said this: 'Citizenship, like anything else, has to be learned. Young people do not become good citizens by accident any more than they become good nurses or good engineers, and learning about citizenship ought to be a dynamic process within our community.' We are now actively promoting the teaching of citizenship within our schools, and this should help children learn to grow up in a society which cares and offers a proper quality of opportunity, but which also offers them an opportunity to take part in the democratic process.

I am very pleased that we are doing this because, in my judgement, we have gone backwards rather than forwards compared to the kind of education in citizenship specifics that I received when I was at school in the 1950s. I am appalled during every election when I go round and talk to young people and find out that it is not that they are uninterested in the electoral process, because often they are (they have become interested through their parents, or the school is running mock elections), but they are ignorant of what is happening. They are ignorant even of the basics – how to go into a polling station and put a cross against their name – even though there are many young people at school who are over the age of 18 and who therefore have the right to vote. We have to change that ignorance.

There are some promising initiatives. Two weeks ago, for example, I spoke at the launch of a Practising Citizenship European Parliament Mock Elections project, sponsored by the Federal Trust and the Hansard Society, which will be teaching 14–18-year-olds about European elections and European citizenship. Formal education at school and later in life clearly has a major role to play in creating the idea of a 'good citizen' – but so too do the much broader, more informal ways in which we transmit values.

Back in February, I gave a lecture about the future of law and order. I discussed the importance of informal social control in reducing crime and disorder, and pointed to what I called 'the walk-on-by society'. My remarks caused something of a stir and, while some commentators supported me, some claimed – wrongly – that I was promoting the idea of a nation of 'have-a-go heroes'. One newspaper columnist said my suggestion that we might consider intervening if we saw a group of 11-year-olds bullying a younger child was 'unrealistic to the point of lunacy'. Well, I disagree. Society cannot function properly without that nexus of informal relationships.

What the debate did reveal very vividly was that, whilst many of us would like to be better citizens, some of the time we are not very sure what this may mean in practice. It does not just apply to whether and how we should intervene to stop misbehaving youngsters, but to a wide range of other situations too, from first-aid emergencies to helping someone out after they have lost a close relative or partner. Afraid of saying or doing the wrong thing, we may end up doing nothing at all. It is something particular about the way we English behave, I think, especially in relation to bereavement and many other situations involving loss. It is not that people do not want to help, it is just that they feel paralysed into inaction.

I do not want to suggest that it is all bad, however, because it is not. Most people require no such urging. There are 6 million people who already care for a relative – child or parent, wife or husband. Millions more do some kind of voluntary work: 350,000 people serve as school governors; 80,000 are involved in residents' associations; an estimated 10 million people are involved in 155,000 Neighbourhood Watch schemes. In all, almost half the population say that they have taken part in some form of voluntary activity in the past year.

What is frustrating when you meet people involved in voluntary activity, however, is that they often express the wish that they had done it earlier. Just this afternoon I went to Earl Road and Tunstall Street in the Smithdown ward of Liverpool to talk to a group of people who were brought together by a Neighbourhood Watch scheme. They have put in some gates in the alleys, and it is proving to be a cheap and very effective form of crime control. It was interesting to hear that these women (they were all women, with one exception) had been living cheek by jowl in a couple of streets, but they had not met each other until they were brought together under the aegis of Neighbourhood Watch. They expressed regret about this, and wished they had got together before. Even with those people who are already involved in voluntary activity, there is huge potential to develop this more.

Voluntary community activity self-evidently brings people together. It helps to create and foster a sense of citizenship which is often missing from our communities today. It can bring in the excluded and enable them to participate in their community: local people working on an environmental art project to brighten up their neighbourhood; tenants working with local authorities to improve street lighting; parents building a new playground where their children can play safely. These initiatives benefit everyone. By participating in these activities, people develop mutual respect for one another as individuals and for society as a whole. Above all, they develop self-confidence and self-respect. I think that is one of the most uplifting things that results from voluntary activity. It is not just what it does for those who are receiving the benefit of the activity, it is also what it does for those doing the giving. I can think of so many occasions when I have been round one of the written-off and run-down estates or inner city areas. I see people whose own lives have been crushed by their environment but who, by being encouraged into voluntary activity – not paid – have suddenly started to walk tall and see some purpose in their lives.

As a Government, we are committed to supporting and promoting this kind of active citizenship. We want to increase the participation of people who until now have not been as involved as others in volunteering, and we want to channel their enthusiasm in productive and satisfying ways. In January this year, the Prime Minister set out a millennium challenge to mark the new century with an explosion of giving. We are doing our best to give that a helping hand. A working group under the chairmanship of Lord Warner is already taking this agenda forward.

The group is drawn from a variety of backgrounds, including voluntary organizations, business and broadcasters, and it is developing a three- to five-year strategy for increasing public involvement in community life. This is the New Active Community Unit, established earlier this month. It is going to work across government, joining up the different things we are doing. It is going to be outward-looking and will include people from outside government as well as inside.

As we enter the next decade, I hope that we, as a people, start to develop a stronger sense of citizenship, a stronger sense of the civil, political and social rights for which our ancestors struggled so hard. Lord Weatherill said in 1990, 'Citizenship is a cultural achievement, a gift of history, which can also be lost or destroyed.' I think we have to nurture citizenship and, in doing so (I make no bones about my communitarian leanings on this), we should not forget that it is not just rights which go with citizenship, but responsibilities and obligations as well. We have duties to do our best for our children, to undertake jury service, to respect the peace and quiet of our neighbours – a hundred and one things that make citizenship a virtue as well as an entitlement and a reward. Citizenship used to be something worth fighting for. Some of the people in Merseyside fought for it, although they may never have realized what they were fighting for at the time. Citizenship today is certainly something worth preserving, and celebrating as well.

THE WAY WE LIVE NOW

Sara Parkin

29 APRIL 1999

Sara Parkin is the Director of Forum for the Future and a Trustee of Friends of the Earth.

As we enter millennium number three, it is a good opportunity to pause in the very hectic pace at which most of us lead our lives to reflect on what we mean by the term citizenship. In the political tradition stemming from the Greek city states and the Roman republic, citizenship has meant involvement in public life by those who have the rights of citizens. In modern times, Liverpool, as a City of Learning, is setting a good example to its citizens by emphasizing that learning is for and about life, about how we take our place in society and in our community in the fullest sense. Both then and now, citizenship means more than just voting now and again.

I would like to expand even further the notion of citizenship and explore the idea of citizenship in a global context – thinking about how we are performing as citizens of the earth from the perspective of time and space and our inner selves. If we are going to develop an idea of modern citizenship that will serve us in both an inspirational and a very practical sense in the next century and in the next millennium, it is essential that we understand more deeply where we fit in temporally, physically and spiritually. I would contend we have lost that deep connection in all three dimensions, which is why we now have to reinvent the notion of good citizenship.

Long before Cicero was writing about the Greek state, there must have been multitudinous codes or sets of rules – written and unwritten – making it easier for people to rub along together, or to collaborate for some common purpose. On a recent visit to Tanzania, I saw the fossilized footprints of a two-billion-year-old family, the oldest on record. It was impossible not to reflect on them as part of some tribe or community, with rituals and even values, most probably geared to increase the likelihood of survival, and certainly developed from the experience of previous generations.

Looking back from the end of the twentieth century, on the cusp of the twenty-first, it is quite interesting to reflect on what has happened over the last hundred years. Each of the 6.3 billion citizens of the planet today will recall different things, but here in the United Kingdom we might reflect on two world wars, the assassination of President Kennedy, the first man on the moon, the Cold War and the collapse of communism. Technologically speaking, we would remember the invention of silicon chips, PCs, Walkmans, heart pacemakers, the splitting of the atom and the gene, perhaps even tamagotchis.

Go back to 1900. What might people looking back over the previous century have reflected upon then? Perhaps the first use of the word 'socialism', George Stephenson's Rocket on the Liverpool–Manchester line, the American Civil War and the abolition of slavery, in which William Roscoe played a significant role. Or perhaps the invention of zips, telephones and, indeed, Coca-Cola.

So much has happened in the last hundred years. So much in such a short time, compared to the speed of change for our ancient ancestors.

If we think in millennia, we can take a different perspective. Many of us may know somebody who is a hundred years old. In a thousand years, however, empires have time to rise and fall, and golden ages can become dark ages and vice versa, of course. At the dawn of the year 1000, there were about 265 million people on this planet, not even double the 170 million people we believe were around when Jesus Christ was born. The number of citizens of this earth of ours, therefore, has gone from 170 million to 6,300 million in 2,000 years. In just 50 more years we expect the number to rise by half again to 9,500 million. As we enter the third millennium, that fact alone is sufficient reason for thinking about citizenship in a global sense. What will people alive in 2100 reflect back upon?

Also, a mere thousand years ago, Western Christendom was emerging from a beleaguered and insignificant backwater of Europe – at least, that is how it was described in my history book. Most people alive then would not have had the foggiest idea that a millennial moment of any sort was taking place, or they might have subscribed to a different faith that operated on a completely different timescale. I believe this year Buddha will be celebrating his 2,563rd birthday, and Mohammed his 1,430th. Yet, nevertheless, the Christian faith now not only dominates the global calendar, but shapes its major institutions. The World Bank and the International Monetary Fund are not known protagonists of Buddhist economics. NATO does not take a Gandhian approach to nonviolent conflict resolution. The grouping of the world's richest nations, the Organization for Economic Co-operation and Development (OECD), has only Turkey and Japan as predominantly non-Christian members. Despite the fact that it has less than a quarter of the world's citizens, the OECD generates three-quarters of the world's trade and uses half the world's energy.

So, as we step into the third millennium, with human progress going global in economic, environmental and technological terms, it seems right to ask whether we have made a good fist of being good citizens of the earth. I say 'we' with emphasis, because there has been a trend towards 'armchair punditry', what somebody called the 'Parker Knoll theory of life'. We are fond of sitting back and pointing accusing fingers at politicians, bureaucrats, captains of industry, banks, churches, seats of learning, newspaper editors – all the people whom we claim run society on our behalf. But we are not separate from them. By electing them (or choosing not to participate in an election), by financing them with our taxes, by buying their products, by studying or worshipping at their feet, or by reading their books and their papers, we make ourselves responsible for the world that they create.

A while ago I looked at some of the visionary work that had been done with young people and with various community groups who had engaged in the Agenda 21 process – the action plan set up by the Earth Summit in 1992 to engage local citizens in their communities in environmental and social issues. I came up with a shortlist of six things that people say they really want.

1 *Ecological security.* An environment that is non-threatening and reasonably predictable.
2 *Systems of justice and government that can be trusted.*
3 *Appropriate technology.* Most are comfortable with high technology, but not the sort that is dangerous or jeopardizes jobs.
4 *Satisfying work.* Work that is satisfying in the sense of being rewarding and varied. People want to be able to fulfil their potential, and are often multi-talented, but unable to use all their talents in their job.
5 *Safe, convivial and supportive communities.* Where success is celebrated and there is support in hard times, and freedom from conflict and war.
6 *A shared sense of purpose and common values.* Despite falling attendance at church, the need for community – in a social as well as a spiritual sense – remains a priority for many.

While this list emerged from research done over the last decade, I reckon it is very close to what our ancestors wanted too. What seems to have gone wrong is that we have not yet worked out a sustainable way of achieving it. We are finding it a real struggle to implement fairly basic and widespread ideas of how people would like their lives to be.

Instead, we seem to have got what Herman Daly, an American environmental economist, has described as a 'full world'. It is estimated that, each year, the global human economy uses between 40 and 50 per cent of the land's biological product – all those resources that are ostensibly renewed each year. That sounds reasonable, but we have to remember that we are taking the half of these resources which is easiest to come by. There are other species that need to share it if they are to survive (and they are key to maintaining stable ecological systems). Moreover, each year, a growing chunk of those renewable resources becomes non-renewable, as, for example, fertile soil is destroyed through deforestation and ill-advised agricultural techniques.

Here in the rich West, we are already experiencing the consequences of reaching the limits of the earth to meet our material demands. The impact of our current levels of consumption on our health, for example, is visible through the rise in childhood asthma and other diseases that prey on weakened immune systems, and the hormone-replicating substances which are thought to be causing the dramatic drop in male fertility. The precise cause or causes are difficult to be sure about, though they are more likely to be a cocktail of reasons than one single one. We know we have a complex and global problem, for example, when we find pesticides produced here in Europe in the snows of the Arctic and the Antarctic.

The impact on our economy is significant too. Not only are there the clean-up bills from past contamination of land, but we are now seeing huge bills coming in for quite unexpected and increasingly frequent extremes of climate. The insurance companies – the big reinsurance companies who are the final stop for the insurance industry – are writing reports that sound like radical tracts from the Green Party. They are concerned because many claims for billions of dollars are being put in each year. Five years ago, on my insurance policy for my house, an 'extra premium' was added for what they called 'natural events' – subsidence from drought, the consequences of flooding, and so on. The consequences of these quite extraordinary and increasingly frequent extreme climatic events are being felt not just in the global economy (and the insurance industry globally is as large as the fossil fuel industry), but right down to the level of domestic insurance.

The impacts of environmental degradation, with the associated social and economic breakdown, are stimulating an increasing number of Foreign Secretaries to make speeches and develop policies. For example, Western Europe, one of the most densely populated regions of the world, is hugely dependent on imports of basic resources. International and internal refugees, fleeing collapsing environments, now far outnumber the 'officially' defined refugees – those escaping political or other persecution.

It was this sort of environmental, economic and social evidence that prompted the United Nations to host a conference in Rio de Janeiro in 1992. The main purpose of what became known as the Earth Summit was to explore the apparent conflict between maintaining a life-supporting environment for the world's citizens and meeting their aspirations in terms of human development. The term 'sustainable development' became the overarching policy goal through which over 170 governments agreed to address the problem.

Despite being possibly the worst sound-bite that any group of people could be lumbered with, sustainable development is not really very difficult to understand. 'Sustainable' just means something that has the capacity for continuance. The challenge therefore is to find a path for human development/progress/ civilization, and the right political arrangement in terms of citizenship and states (or however we want to describe the place we live), that can deliver satisfaction and wellbeing to all, but which does not destroy the capacity of our environment to support life in the meantime.

And we should make no mistake about it: equity – fairness – is at the heart of sustainability. Although we in Britain and Europe live in a very sophisticated civilization in many technological senses, the basic ingredients of citizenship are not available to the majority of people on earth. A fifth of the world's population is hungry (while another fifth suffers from a different form of malnutrition, obesity) and 2 billion people are described by the World Bank as 'water insecure'. Even in the OECD, about 40 per cent of sewage goes raw into the sea. Despite the world being richer than ever, the gap between the richest and the poorest is widening: you can see it happening in the United Kingdom and you can see it happening globally.

In Tanzania, I visited hospitals and was humbled at how much is done with virtually no resources at all to care for people who are sick. The contrast with, say, a hospital in Liverpool is stark. In this City of Learning, there is a commitment to learning for all, with new technologies enabling access to information and learning materials in a truly extraordinary way. Yet, while there are supposed to be about eight books per person in the world (which comes to about 50 billion books), a quarter of the world's population still cannot read or write. In Tanzania, gifts of pencils and biros are craved because an enormous number of children cannot even learn the basics as they do not have pens to write with or paper to write on.

Can we here in Europe really call ourselves any sort of citizens when so many people are being denied such basic ingredients of civilization?

If anything is to change, a top priority must be a reformulation of *our* perceptions of *our* own responsibilities. We need to look again at the whole balance of citizenship between rights and responsibilities. Where do we fit in on this earth? Where do we belong? Where is home? What are our obligations to the place where we are and to each other? I agree 100 per cent with the emphasis on responsibility, because my experience (in other countries as well as here in Britain) is that rights are no use without a mechanism for delivering them. And the only *sustainable* delivery mechanism is our feeling that it is our responsibility. If you are in a society where there is a shared sense of responsibility to deliver rights, then you have them. If there is no responsibility, then you do not have the rights.

I believe that it is an intrinsic part of our humanity to do right by others and the place where we live. Maybe it is just a piece of the evolutionary memory that we have lost or have been separated from by the helter-skelter pace of human progress over the last few centuries. Certainly, judging from the way we have constructed our idea of progress and what is right, we have had to bury those basic instincts. The relevant MORI polls and work done exploring basic values in young children reveal that the majority have no difficulty in understanding instinctively what is right and what is wrong. Yet we seem to live and work in a society that does not reward such instincts at the moment.

I would like to look a little more closely now at how we might develop a new idea of citizenship. And perhaps the best way to explain what I mean is through my own experience. I was a typical 1960s teenager. My prime concern was monitoring the transition between the age of jazz and the age of the Beatles. My parents told me they had sacrificed their youth in the war, and therefore I had a responsibility to have a good time. I took this responsibility really seriously. The political message was that we had never had it so good. There was no unemployment, so it did not matter if you fooled around at university and took an extra year because jobs were not a problem.

At that time, I was studying to be a nurse. We learnt how the human body works. It is made up mostly of water, and is essentially a pile of chemicals. Our molecules are in a state of constant change and renewal, so after about six years every molecule in our body has probably changed. If, therefore, you were to turn to your wife after seven years of marriage and say, 'I'm not the person you married,' physically speaking you could be absolutely right! It is not just the food we eat that gives us a relationship with the environment. We are in a permanent, intimate physical engagement with it. Yet how many people know this scientific fact? How many people understand that we are literally 'of our environment'? What we do to it, we do to ourselves.

In the 1960s we also witnessed the first pictures of the earth taken from the moon. It was an amazing experience for many people, including me. You could see the edges of the place in which we lived. There was, to all intents and purposes, nowhere else to go except the earth. And it was beautiful – that was also something quite extraordinary, to see it all, and to see that it was beautiful. At a cellular level, the world is extraordinarily beautiful too. Although we had the technology to put a man on the moon then, it is only very recently that serious research has been undertaken into the way the systems of the earth work – those that affect the climate, recycle wastes and provide oxygen, for example. There has been some fascinating work recently that suggests that micro-organisms in the sea are actually using the wind to blow them off the crests of the waves and up into the clouds. Somewhat heretically, I have wondered if the World Wildlife Fund should exchange its panda symbol for a mug of blue-green algae – an organism that probably has a much bigger role to play in the sustainability of life on earth.

It is hard to explain why so little research has been done into the way the world 'works' until recent evidence (mostly from the climate) that it was not working as well as it should. We have spent a fortune on research into nuclear technologies and genetic technologies, the tiny building blocks of life, but have demonstrated a singular lack of curiosity about how they all fit together and operate at a systematic level. In Edinburgh in 1789, however, a certain James Hutton (a contemporary of William Roscoe), who was a physician, a farmer and a philosopher, did describe the whole earth as one organism. He said it was a little like the way the body works, and that the actual purpose of the earth was life itself. That was at a time when the microscope was all the rage, so Hutton's view was not popular then, just as

William Roscoe was terribly brave in maintaining (however difficult it was and whatever personal consequences it had for him) that slavery was not right. Now, at last, we have reached the stage with the climate scientists where we are really starting to understand, not only the incredible power of our world, but also the fragility of the mechanisms and the consequences of our interventions.

The other thing I learnt about this time was how disconnected our society, our politics and our economics are from what I saw as the scientific realities of the way the world worked and the way we fitted into it. Biologically we were of the environment rather than separate from it, yet economically and politically it seemed this connection did not exist. In 1971 a paper, written, ironically, by a NASA space scientist discussed the thermo-dynamics of pollution. It pointed out the scientific truth that energy and raw materials, when passing through the human economy, change in form. A piece of coal, for example, when burnt, delivers heat to the economy, but is changed to ash, carbon dioxide, sulphur dioxide and so on. The same chemicals go in, but they come out of the burning process in a different form – which, if produced in large quantities, pollutes the environment. Yet the cost of dealing with the pollution is not captured in the cost of the coal. It is paid through the health budget, or in reparations for dying trees etc.

We operate in an economy based on a theory that assumes that there is no connection between the exchange of money, the use of raw materials and the consequences of producing pollution. It assumes raw materials and energies are dirt cheap or, in some cases, free, and that the powerful and sophisticated waste treatment service of the natural world can be taken for granted. It encourages and rewards profligacy in resource use and waste generation.

The best example of how grave this is comes from the United Kingdom's waste industry itself. It is estimated that each year every person in Britain buys about 1,000 kg of 'stuff'. Half is food, the rest things like clothes, cars, records, furniture and so on. In order to bring that 1,000 kg of 'stuff' to the shops, 10,000 kg of energy and material is mobilized. That is to say, for every 1,000 kg we pay for, another 10,000 kg of water, rocks, lorries, energy etc., has to be used. By and large, we do not pay for this – the bill is picked up elsewhere, in the health of people in other countries and in the consequences to the environment. Moreover, it is estimated that after six months, only 100 kg of the stuff we bought is left in our homes.

Resource Productivity – the Practical Challenge
Biffa, 1999

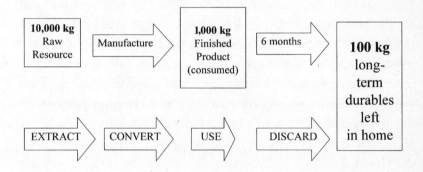

It has been calculated that if we want to achieve sustainability, in a way that is fair to all people, then we need to reduce our resource consumption – that annual 'take' of the land's resources – by around 90 per cent. Sounds impossible. Yet, if you say to energy and material scientists, 'We've got this problem: we'd like very much to lead a comfortable life of high quality for all the world's citizens, but here is evidence that we can't go on consuming the energy and raw materials as we are doing because the consequences are so serious to the environment,' they reply, 'You want 90 per cent improvement in efficiency and use of energy and materials? *Technically*, that's no problem. There's no difficulty in being much more thrifty in the way we use energy and raw materials. It can be done. We're extremely profligate and we haven't had to worry about that before.' So the real problem, then, is not technical, but economic and political, as we measure the success of our civilization largely through increases of its 'output' of goods and services. Until we change that, being ten times more productive with resources will remain more a dream than a reality.

But there are signs of hope. The present Government is beginning to put in place some environmental taxes, with the idea of making the price of goods and services more environmentally and ethically 'right'. Thus, when you buy something or when you do something, the amount you pay for it actually brings on board the real cost of its impact on other people and on the environment. Some leading companies are beginning to think about this too – not least because companies that survive are the ones that can think what the market will be like twenty years from now, and position themselves accordingly. One of the partners working with Forum for the Future is a company called Interface, one of Europe's biggest carpet manufacturers. They have said that twenty years from now people will be leasing floor coverings, because really, when you think about it, we do not truly want to *own* the carpet. What we want is a warm, attractive floor covering, and so the company says they will take responsibility for the carpet. They will lease it to us, and when it wears out or when we move, they will take it back and lease us another one. So we would rent it rather than buy it, and the company would take responsibility for closing the loop so that there is absolutely minimum input of energy and raw materials in carpets. They would make old carpets the resource that provides new ones.

There are other companies beginning to think of this too. It is quite true that we do not really want to own a washing machine that goes rusty and falls apart after five years, but we would like to have the capacity to get our clothes clean. We do not really want energy either. What we want is heat, light and power, and companies like BP are beginning to rethink themselves to develop new solar technologies on a scale to make a serious difference. They know they are going to have to change if we choose, or are forced to choose (and I think the whole point about citizenship is that it should be the former rather than the latter), to lead our lives, buy things and do things in a way that is hugely more resource and energy efficient.

Why are we not doing this very fast, then? Well, there is a little problem. Politicians actually do want to deliver what people want, and we want them to deliver what we want. They appear, however, *structurally* incapable of doing it. We may want a social democracy, with a worthwhile sort of citizenship and protection for the environment, but we are unlikely to achieve that when we also have a global economic market which rewards profligacy and ruthless competition – measuring value in monetary terms only. It certainly does not reward people for *not* employing children in sweat shops, for example, and is a poor policeman of environmental vandalism. If we accept that sort of economy as the only sort we can have, it will never serve us by helping to deliver the quality and standards we want for our environment, the way we run our societies and how we relate to each other. Another Roscoe contemporary, Adam Smith, described the invisible hand of the market, but also pointed out that this should be shaped by the values and beliefs of citizens.

I agree with Peter Toyne, who said that the sort of citizenship we are talking about here has to be *learnt*. As a species – and again this is something I reflected on in Tanzania – we are undeniably tribal. We have not developed physically and psychologically at the same pace as our economies and technologies. We are simply not used to living cheek by jowl with each other. Western Europe is one of the most densely populated places in the world. Successful human relationships have always depended on a range of negotiated compromises in order to achieve the maximum of our common objectives – objectives that tolerate, but which are not unwarrantably derailed by, legitimate minority points of view. Such continuing negotiations about common objectives and legitimate minority points of view are the stuff of families. They are the stuff of communities. They are the stuff of international bodies. They are absolutely the stuff of citizenship – it is a dynamic process, not a static one.

In the United Kingdom, grossly inadequate democratic arrangements and the cult of the selfish individual as the only economic factor worth considering have removed this sort of debate from public life for too long. We should have a culture in which we continually debate those areas – what is right and wrong, what is good and bad, what we want to do together, and how we tolerate others. That has to be part and parcel of the things we learn, and it is great that the whole subject is going to be brought into schools. I just hope it will be extended from the traditional approach to citizenship as just being in relation to the State. I want it enlarged to be in relation to the whole earth. I think there are some really exciting opportunities ahead to make up for all the lost time and discover a genuinely fulfilling and fair civilization in the new millennium.

People's civic energy is not dead. It may be dozing, and people have understandably disengaged from local democratic participation in particular. In Britain, however, more than in all the other Western European countries, this has resulted in a kaleidoscope of socially entrepreneurial groups. A survey has suggested that, for every 100,000 people in Britain, there are 300 of these groups. They deliver about 400,000 full-time jobs, which is about 2 per cent of the workforce. They contribute over £12 billion to the GNP. We do not hear about this in the statistics, but all these tiny groups do exist and they have been well documented. About 4 million people engage in some voluntary activity at least once a month. Birmingham looked at local socially entrepreneurial groups and found that, for every £1 the council put in, they actually mobilized £4 of matching funding for what they were doing, for example working with old people.

These groups are delivering on the ground the sort of services that are not being delivered by our funding- and power-parched local authorities.

If this Government does not delay too much the whole process of democratization that is starting in Scotland, but moves it on quite fast to the English regions, then the opportunities to channel this local energy into sustainable regeneration are huge. At present, there are lots of things happening, but progress is really handicapped by the fact that there is not sufficient regional and local empowerment available. People have stopped their innovation and entrepreneurism because they do not have what they need in terms of local finance and local partnerships. The ideas are there, nonetheless.

There is, in addition, an urgent need to do something to slow and reverse environmental degradation. This challenge offers a very powerful focus for thinking about what we need to do in more complicated times. At the end of the Cold War, when the ideological battle which had shaped the view of the world for so many people for so long ended, we also realized that the glue, the common set of values, that kept society together had been dissolving for a long time. People were left a little bit adrift, not quite sure what to do. This morning on *Thought for the Day*, the speaker pointed out that the churches of all denominations had a lot to answer for, for not making themselves relevant to people's lives and the issues of today (there are exceptions, of course). It is quite clear, certainly, that the churches are not leading the debate on what the next millennium needs in terms of common purposes and values – they are just tagging along a bit, which is regrettable.

I think the environment also has a very positive role to play at a diplomatic level, both in fractured communities and internationally as a means to resolving engrained conflicts. If you look at diplomatic theory, and are trying to bring two sides together, who perhaps have a track record of hatred between them lasting for generations, then the starting point is to find one piece of common ground. Once both sides are on that common ground, the idea is to work out from there. What could be a more powerful piece of common ground than the shared need for a life-supporting environment? However many members of my family you may have killed, whatever the colour of his skin or her religion, we each need exactly the same standard of life-supporting environment – in our communities and globally. What could be a better way of bringing people together at an international level for peace-building? Israelis and Palestinians, for example, could eventually come together because they share a common water resource, and if they do not collaborate over it, neither can survive.

The environment can also intercede at a very direct personal level. We have all heard about the disaffected children from dysfunctional families, or otherwise alienated from their communities, who are sometimes (not enough) taken off on adventure trips, to do white-water rafting in France for example. At one time this seemingly inappropriate 'holiday' generated a lot of negative publicity. Yet the experience, which was carefully constructed and professionally led, helped these boys to understand how the natural world works, and how social groups work better together as a team. They learnt about the power of the water, the wildness of the area, and what they had to do to raft down a river successfully, put up a tent and cook a meal. Through building a relationship with the natural world the boys learnt to build a relationship with other people, and in the process, recover their self-esteem and find confidence in the fact that they could take decisions that affect their own future in a positive way.

The back end of this millennium has seen some pretty monstrous experiments with 'isms' – Marxism, Thatcherism, socialism, fascism, and so on. All of them have denied critical parts of our humanity and all of them have totally disregarded the environment. None have been adequate for our purposes, or for the challenge of ensuring that environmental sustainability and human development move forward together rather than in conflict as they do at the moment.

It is not an illusion to believe that we can achieve our potential as individuals and improve the quality of life for all people without damaging the capacity of our environment to support life. We need to re-link our ideas of citizenship to our deep physical and spiritual relationship with and responsibility to our planet. If we can do this, then I think we will not only be able to see our responsibility to each other and to future generations, but also understand the satisfaction and pleasure there is to be had in fulfilling those responsibilities.

A CULTURE OF CITIZENSHIP

Melvyn Bragg

4 FEBRUARY 2000

Lord Bragg of Wigton is the presenter and editor of The South Bank Show. *He is the Chancellor of Leeds University and is the author of many books and screenplays. He was created a Life Peer in 1998.*

This is an immense subject, which brings both advantages and disadvantages. It means that I can rove into the wild blue yonder and still feel that I am somewhere near the subject – after all, citizenship and the millennium are vast vats, full of possible meanings. It compels generalization; it provokes grand, even wild, assertions. I intend to yield to those temptations.

What I want to do is to look first at the landscape of the world we live in now, and then to see if I can fit citizenship into any pattern that emerges. I feel rather like Aladdin letting the genie out of the lamp – the genie is our new millennium, and citizenship can perhaps be compared to getting that overpowering genie back into the lamp.

It is important, I think, to attempt to create a map of where we are, however sketchy and patchy it is, because citizenship – our place in the world and our responsibilities to the world – can only be understood in context. The citizens of ancient, classical Athens understood their role, especially in relation to women, slaves and lower orders, none of whom, of course, were deemed to be 'citizens'. That elite idea about citizens was sustained for a very long time wherever there were cities, and for long periods there were very few cities of note. Only comparatively recently – since the French and American Revolutions, for instance – did the idea of the citizen as we know it emerge from the crowd. The time, the population size, the economy, the level of material, intellectual and human progress, were right at last. Since then, our concept of citizenship has developed, ensuring that even the lower classes, women, former slaves and former colonized people are included. Now it is beginning to reach out its hand to young people too. The rise of the citizen – never unchallenged – is one of the great and most optimistic stories of the modern age.

So where does the citizen stand in this expanding, revolutionary, unpredictable, awesomely intelligent new world or new millennium?

If power really is moving away from government to globally effective companies whose net worth is often bigger than that of the nations – and not only developing nations, but developed nations too – and if the very essence of citizenship is its relationship to power, then there is a problem. What power does the *citizen* have inside or outside a company? Consumers have power; shareholders have power; executives have power; that ever-growing millennium monster the market has power. But you and I, what power do we have? Can we vote them in or vote them out? Can we pass laws making these companies suitable to our own culture of working practices, sick leave, maternity leave, pensions, minimum wage?

Well, we *can*, but if they dislike it they can relocate, as so many American and British companies do. Bangalore in Southern India is one of the fastest growing countries of our new world in technological terms. The people are intelligent, their brain power is excellent, but above all the wages are 15 per cent less than the wages in Texas. So Texas ups stumps to Bangalore. All global companies can relocate like this, and they are the new power barons. There will surely be a showdown, probably a series of showdowns, in which the state and the politicians are forced to act on behalf of the traditional right of democratic citizens.

The warlords of ancient China come to mind in any analysis of this sort, as do the overweening barons of medieval England. You cannot have effective citizenship if the power which pays the piper and calls the tune is not invested in citizenship in any way. Global business is a different game in which votes, issues and constitutions apply only so far as they help the company's efficiency and no further.

This is not to say that business is bad. It is not. It has brought enormous benefit to mankind, especially in the last few centuries. It cannot, however, really be expected to be interactive with what does not contribute to its drive, focus and *raison d'être* – i.e. with full and democratic citizenship. Politics looks after that, but politicians need power to be effective. Consumer groups, capitalist vigilantes, global guerrillas – they are already in existence, in some form. These are the avant-garde, strong for citizenship, alive to the struggle.

The third millennium citizen will need to be a very clued-up economic animal. He or she will also need to be able to carry several passports at once. We will all be part of multiple communities as never before. We have been prepared for this. We have belonged over the ages to Church and State, to local and national communities. We have often had great difficulty in maintaining these several allegiances – when our Church was opposed to our State, or when our local community was at odds with our national community. Then, as now, there were divisions and contradictions which often ran deep.

How much deeper do they run now? We are all part of many communities: of cities like Liverpool; of England; of the United Kingdom; of Europe, too, to a considerable extent; of the North Atlantic Treaty Organization; of the United Nations; of any number of private interest groups; and, as I indicated above, possibly of organizations where allegiances can float like a butterfly and sting like a bee. You can be in the northeast of England and yet your first loyalty can be to Japan, which pays your wages and can guarantee a future. Citizens of Bangalore have their Texan dependence as well as their loyalty to India, and at any time the two might be in opposition. The simple citizen, therefore, is no longer with us.

Democracy in which the citizen flourished has worked well in some nation states, but how does a citizen keep a grip on democracy, keep it in good order, keep it fit for the struggle to stay alive, when so many short cuts and price cuts threaten to bypass it? That seems to me to be the nub of the issue. Here I am no prophet at all. What I urge is that we first hold on to what we have. We cannot defend what we do not practise. We cannot expand what we do not exercise.

Democracy can mean many things to different people and will continue to do so. What can we do? We can do simple things. Vote when you are of age. Read the stuff they push through your letterbox – or some of it, anyway. Those who always carry the cause may persuade others of a policy for the future. Look again at the history of what has been done to raise up so many over the years, so that now we enjoy rights, freedom, opportunities – and realize what a recent and fragile enterprise this is. Do not be afraid to take part in politics. Party politics is not a fashionable pursuit at the moment, but it has rarely been more vital that committed and bright-eyed people maintain the exhausting task of keeping the idea of citizenship alive.

Being a good citizen in today's world means both obeying the law and, in a democracy, challenging the law if you think it is wrong. It is not easy in a country such as ours, where so much has already been done and where, comparatively speaking, there is so much to rest on. It is not easy to see the urgency, not easy to decide whether the effort is worth it. Nonetheless, unless some, at least, of the strongest in each generation are prepared to take on a political role, the great idea of equal citizenship in a democracy will crumble and decay, like a neglected church. The price of liberty is eternal vigilance. The price of citizenship in a century hurtling into new extremes, more like a comet than a planet, is no less high. Unless we use it, actively use our citizenship, we will surely lose it. It has probably never been so difficult to fathom the future. More praise, then, to those who attempt it.

Finally, we must surely also *train* more for citizenship. There is so much of a burden thrown on teachers already that it is unfair to expect them to do much more, but surely citizenship must be seen as a key to the running and maintenance of our democracy. How are we to guard and develop it unless by learning? Each generation needs to learn that dictatorships, however they came about, will finally grind down as many people as they can. Each generation needs to learn that a full and rich life for all begins in the health of the state or region, and this is dependent on the determination of those who support it. We have to be very careful. Democracy may be no more than a slip of history unless we tend to it. As we saw in the last century, it has plenty of enemies. Single-issue groups – local, national and international – are most vividly experiencing citizenship now, often to great effect. That is to be applauded, but they need an army of the rest of us behind them.

One thing is certain about this new century and new millennium: the knowledge-holders will be in control over empires of which the Romans could never have dreamed. Like all previous elites, however, the knowledge-holders will want their own way. It is very easy to envisage a world of massive privilege held by the few, with the rest numerically superior but chastened, abused and drugged to subjugation, deprived non-players, non-citizens. We have, after all, been there before.

The crux of it is this: the more control the more of us have, the less we can be exploited. I am not a Marxist and, indeed, if any single message informs my own thinking, it is the most radical message in 20 centuries of preaching, the Sermon on the Mount itself. We must, however, be on the alert now that the knowledge-rich and *only* they, their corporations and communities inherit the earth. The only force which can bring them *down* to earth is that of educated, decent and determined citizens – of which this country has so far had its proud and inspiring share.

CHRISTIANITY AND CITIZENSHIP

George Carey

23 FEBRUARY 2000

The Most Revd Dr George Carey has been the Archbishop of Canterbury since 1991. He was previously the Bishop of Bath and Wells (1987–91).

The Foundation for Citizenship owes much to Lord Alton and his colleagues, and to Liverpool John Moores University. Indeed, David Alton has provided much useful food for thought with his recent book *Citizen Virtues*. The emphasis of the Foundation, however, is not just on thinking and talking about citizenship, but also on trying to foster it, to produce good citizens. Although there is much to celebrate here, I think it is fair to say that the impetus for this very impressive body of work on citizenship was less a sense of celebration than a sense of crisis – a sense that in Liverpool, as in so many places, the glue that binds societies together was in danger of losing its adhesive power. There were too many people feeling left out rather than included, worthless rather than valued, hurting rather than fulfilled.

That, as many will know, was also an important part of the message of the hugely influential report *Faith in the City*, which the Church of England produced in the mid-1980s. That report formed the foundation for the Church Urban Fund, which has done a great deal of work in urban areas across the country. Some people greeted *Faith in the City* with hostility, regarding it virtually as a Marxist tract. It was no such thing, but it was certainly prophetic, both in describing the problem and in suggesting ways of tackling it.

As I will seek to illustrate, the Christian approach to many of the issues surrounding citizenship has a long history, and one biased towards practical involvement. Making a priority of citizenship, it seems to me, is an important part of trying to regain what has been lost, of building something better in which more people can share a sense of belonging and self-worth.

Actually, the term 'citizen' – to me at least – is not one that sits very easily on English ears. There is Citizen Kane, if you are a film buff; or Citizen Smith, if your taste runs to ageing sitcoms. It is not a very extensive set of references, is it? A different context is offered by the Citizens Advice Bureau. That has certainly proved a valuable resource, especially when we need to get advice on our rights – our rights as citizens. These are rights that a distinguished son of Liverpool, William Gladstone, helped to shape, of course, through his commitment to parliamentary and other reform in the nineteenth century. (Incidentally, being Prime Minister was something of a second best for Gladstone. His original ambition was to be a Church of England clergyman!)

Rights are important and must never be taken for granted. A society that fails to respect such rights – human rights, civil rights, legal rights – is not likely to be a very healthy place. Rights cannot be understood on their own, however. They exist and have meaning in a context of responsibilities and obligations. For Christians, our understanding of our rights as citizens is intimately connected to another c-word: our ties to the community.

Nearly 1,600 years ago, St Augustine's great work *City of God* explored both the possibilities and the limitations of human communities – what Augustine calls the 'City of Earth'. Augustine says that we are all in 'exile' in this 'city', yet we are to reach out in hope to something beyond our human limitations. For Augustine, that 'something' is the 'City of God'. 'The freedom of that city,' Augustine writes, 'will be *one single will* present in everyone, freed from all evil and filled with every good, enjoying continually the delight of eternal joy.' Indeed, that is something to look forward to.

Augustine accepts that the city or community of man can never be the Kingdom of God, can never be perfect. Like the quest for an earthly paradise, it is bound to fall short. It is a notion which, from the Garden of Eden right up to the present, continues to tantalize and tease us. The Leonardo DiCaprio film, *The Beach*, for example, deals with just this idea – a paradise on earth that proves to be something rather different. William Golding's influential novel *Lord of the Flies* explores similar terrain. The Christian doctrine of original sin is a statement of the way we fall short of our aspirations, our idealism and our longings for perfection. 'Utopia', after all, means 'no place'. Sir Thomas More's satire on this theme is a reminder to politicians and to us all that a perfect society and perfect citizens will always remain fantasies. We are dealing with ourselves.

In St Augustine, however, the acceptance that human endeavour is flawed is not a dead end or a defeat. Instead, it challenges us to look to the future, and to do so in a special way – in a way that, like some pairs of glasses, is bifocal. We have to keep our sights set both on the short-range, the 'here and now' of our everyday life, and also on the long-range promise of the glorious life that is to come. This life to come is one in which our disparate needs, desires and concerns will be melded together into 'one single will' for good. That future promise is what Christians hope for, certainly, and it is that hope which informs the Christian understanding of how to be a 'citizen' of this 'City of Earth'.

Christianity, community, citizenship: the three c's. How do they fit together in practice? I want to suggest that it comes down to how we relate to others. You do not have to dig very deep into the Christian Gospels to find the ideas of community and relationship powerfully expressed. Christ's injunction to 'love your neighbour as yourself' is not only an exhortation to think beyond ourselves, it also carries the clear implication that, in order to be truly ourselves, we must attend to others as well. The great seventeenth-century poet and Dean of St Paul's Cathedral, John Donne, captured this sense of necessary relationship with others when he wrote, 'No man is an island, entire of itself; every man is a piece of the continent, a part of the main. Any man's death diminishes me, because I am involved in mankind.'

A citizen, therefore, does not just have a tick list of rightful possessions. A citizen also has a necessary set of relations, obligations and responsibilities. Citizenship is not merely about what we should have, it is also about what we should do and how we should do it. It is not only about 'having', but also about 'being'. It has to do with others.

I was in South Africa recently. There is a wonderful African word, *ubuntu*, for which there is no precise English equivalent. Nelson Mandela summed it up in this way: 'It is the sense that we can only be human through the humanity of others.' *Ubuntu*, you could say, means community at its deepest level. For Christians that is modelled in the example of Christ himself. It is a message, of course, which has special resonance in South Africa as its people, with the Churches very much involved, strive to build a new, post-apartheid sense of community. It is no less of a challenge wherever and whoever we are. When you pause to think about it, most of us inhabit, or seek to inhabit, a number of different communities.

To Christian thinking, a crucial one of these is the community of the family. I believe the family is the basic building block of community and citizenship. How we learn to interact with our parents, grandparents, siblings and other relations shapes so much of the values, standards, expectations and obligations by which we live the rest of our lives. That learning process, especially across generations, is not always easy. You may recall Mark Twain's remarks: 'When I was a boy of fourteen, my father was so ignorant I could hardly stand to have the old man around. But when I got to be twenty-one, I was astonished at how much the old man had learnt in seven years.'

Some family problems are less easily and wittily overcome. Indeed, many people would argue that the community of the family is in crisis. The erosion of its shape and stability – reflected in both divorce rates and the undermining of marriage as an institution – impacts on hundreds of thousands of individual lives, many of them young and vulnerable lives. It also places severe strain on the fabric of society. The American academic Francis Fukuyama, in his book, *The Great Disruption*, identifies this erosion as a serious element in the loss of what he calls 'social capital' – the ability to trust and form associations outside the family. This has serious economic and social consequences, for the community of the family helps to shape not only who we are as individuals, but also what we become as citizens – our public as well as our private, our social as well as our personal sense of ourselves.

Of course there are traditional families that are disaster areas, where there is such bitterness between parents that children end up as the spoils of war, damaged and traumatized. Equally, single and divorced parents are no less loving or devoted to their children. Yet research continues to show that marriage provides the most secure and stable environment for children. A secure home offers the best context for the dynamics of love and acceptance, tolerance and understanding, rights and responsibilities, firmness and gentleness, rules and guidelines. That is more likely to generate a healthy bank balance of 'social capital', to use Fukuyama's term, for the potential benefit of all. Certainly, social capital is not a product of most dysfunctional homes. Of course, from a Christian perspective the model of marriage matters not just because it may work better for families and communities, but also because it is part of God's design for us.

That is not to say that Christian or religious communities are perfect. At its best the congregation of a church may be a remarkable support network of people from a range of backgrounds, difficult to match in its diversity in virtually any other context. But congregations can also become inward-looking and exclusive, cut off from the wider world. It is a proud aspiration of the Church of England – and one that I hold dear – that we are not insular, gathered communities of the faithful. We are open to all. A substantial basis, I believe, of our claim to be a national church is that we are there to minister to and serve all who come to us, wherever and whoever they are.

A similar impulse means that we are also called to reach out to other faith communities. Last autumn I initiated a remarkably well attended and supported debate in the House of Lords on the role of religions in promoting a just and peaceful world. I was delighted that David Alton was one of the speakers. In that debate, I took issue with the well-rehearsed idea that religion is a source of endless division and conflict. It has performed that unfortunate role at times, but that is only part of the story. There is now great potential, I believe, for faith communities and leaders to be bridges to understanding and harmony, not barriers and bulwarks of division.

This country is now a very diverse one in terms of cultural and ethnic background. Our neighbours may come from anywhere in the world. They may be from Warrington or Warsaw, Runcorn or Rwanda. They may be Muslim or Christian, Hindu or Buddhist. It is tempting to think that the communal challenges of such diversity are almost entirely modern, but the Christian perspective was defined 2,000 years ago in Jesus' parable of the Good Samaritan. 'Who is my neighbour?' a Jewish lawyer asked Jesus. He responded by telling a story about a Jew making a journey along a rough road. He was attacked, beaten up, robbed, stripped and left for dead. A fellow Jew came along, a priest, as a matter of fact, and he did not want to get involved, so he rushed home. Along came another Jew, a Levite, and he too was rather busy, so he did not bother to stop either. Finally, the Samaritan came along and not only cared for the injured man and took him to an inn, but also paid for his lodging. The point of the story was that the Samaritan was not a Jew and certainly would not have been considered a neighbour. He was very definitely a member of another community – indeed, of a group despised by the Jews at the time. Yet he was the one who reached across the divide.

Of course, breaking down barriers is nothing new to the churches in Liverpool. The co-operation between Anglicans and Roman Catholics is well documented and justly celebrated. David Sheppard and the late Derek Worlock formed a formidable alliance that continues to flourish and develop under their successors, Archbishop Patrick Kelly and Bishop James Jones. It is an alliance based on a vision of a fully engaged Christianity, committed to making a practical difference to the lives of individuals and communities. My distinguished predecessor as Archbishop of Canterbury, William Temple, once said, 'Christianity is the most materialistic of all religions.' In other words, the idea of Christ taking human form expresses God's commitment to the world. God in Christ Jesus was willing to get his hands dirty in the ordinariness of humanity, and so he calls us to action. We are meant to roll up our sleeves and get stuck in, and we are meant to involve others.

The current focus on what has become known as 'social exclusion' reflects this Christian imperative. It is not just about being part of the community ourselves, it is also about bringing in others who feel left out. Those who feel excluded and rejected, useless and unloved, are unlikely to be the most effective citizens. There is a practical as well as a moral imperative here. Social exclusion is related to the idea of social capital which I mentioned earlier. Rejected children, out-of-work young people and aggressive and alienated adults are in no one's interest. People need support and encouragement, but they also need skills and training; they need not only to feel that the door is open, but also that, once inside, they can make a contribution. A sense of personal worth feeds the social capital of communities.

Once again, we find the Christian view of citizenship closely linked to community – in this case the community in which we learn and the community in which we work. It was a similar impulse that first inspired the Church's role in education in this country. It represents a long and proud history of practical community involvement, and one, incidentally, that predates much in the way of government activity. It is not just history, however. Many church schools are very popular today, and rightly so. Parents value the fact that our schools offer sound and stimulating education set in a clear spiritual and moral framework. We look to equip young people not only with skills and knowledge for a job, but also with values for life.

We would like to do more, especially in secondary education. Certainly the demand is there. I am delighted that Lord Dearing is currently leading a review into the possibilities. Today we are partners with government in education, and it is proving to be a positive partnership. The Education Secretary, David Blunkett, has been generous in his praise for what we offer, and receptive to many of our ideas and concerns. It will come as no surprise, given what I have already said about the importance we attach to the family for the wider community, that we believe strong support should be given in schools to marriage as the fundamental building block of family life. I am pleased that ministers have been prepared to listen carefully to our views and priorities in considering a statutory framework for future guidance to schools. In addition, the school curriculum is now to include citizenship itself – the very stuff of this lecture series and the work of the Foundation for Citizenship. It is a development I welcome and one that sits well, I think, with the Church's own focus on prioritizing a moral and ethical context for education.

I am always impressed by Liverpool's openness to the world beyond. The city's great maritime tradition means that it has long been connected to other countries and cultures. Indeed, a city that is twinned with Shanghai could never be accused of excessive introspection! One use of the word 'citizen' I did not mention at the outset is 'citizen of the world'. It strikes me as having a slightly quaint ring to it now – harking back to a time when most of us did not or could not travel all that far, when the world was a largely unexplored idea somewhere over the horizon. Today most of us, I think, have a more sophisticated understanding of the idea and more experience of the reality, both through foreign travel and the fact that we live in an increasingly interconnected and interdependent world. In some instances, this gives us greater variety and diversity – the fruit and vegetables all year round in our supermarkets, for example, can come from virtually anywhere these days. In other cases, however, it means a reduction of that diversity and a greater uniformity, with global brands and products wiping out local variations. Either way, we now have to add the idea of a global community to all the other communities of which we might need or want to be members.

What does this mean for a Christian understanding of citizenship and community? A great deal of my time is spent on the implications of being a member of the global community. Compared with much of the world, we live in a very privileged and wealthy society, where the availability of food and shelter, education and health care are generally taken for granted. Other members of our global community have rather different expectations and experiences: 1.3 billion people live on less than 70 pence a day; a further 3 billion people live on under £1.50; 100 million children die every year of readily treatable diseases. If I am a citizen of the world, I have to care for that world, and for my brothers and sisters who lack the basic necessities of life. This presents us in the West with a moral challenge.

As part of this challenge in recent years, the Churches and many other organizations have taken part in the Jubilee 2000 campaign, which is endeavouring to eliminate the crushing burden of debt that many very poor countries have to pay off. I pay tribute to our Government and in particular the Chancellor, Gordon Brown, and Clare Short, the Secretary of State for International Development, for their personal commitment to making sure that Britain is helping to lead the way on debt reduction. Some other wealthy countries could and should do more. It is important to keep up the pressure, especially if there is a danger of slipping behind schedules already agreed.

Membership of this global community carries a very real set of obligations and responsibilities. Globalization is not only a physical reality, however, it is also a virtual one. I mean, of course, the exponential growth of information technology, especially as manifested by the internet. Increasingly, we are not only citizens of the world but also citizens of the worldwide web. Clearly, the access to information and the ability to tap resources not otherwise available can be a potent tool of empowerment. It can be part of the education for citizenship and participation that I discussed earlier.

It can also be exclusive and isolating, however. 'Only connect!' wrote E.M. Forster memorably in the novel *Howard's End* – but he had something more in mind than a PC with a modem. Of course, you may argue, e-mail can be a way of making important connections. That is true, but it can also be a distorting and unsatisfactory one, in which self-deception and evasion are prominent. The Christian emphasis is on relationships not just connections: yes, we have to make contact, but it is the *quality* of that contact which matters. We must be sure that the virtual community is at the service of the real communities, not a substitute for them. It must be a tool for inclusion, not a weapon of exclusion. In other words, exactly the same values and priorities should obtain in this new community as in the others I have mentioned.

From the nuclear family to cyberspace, what we have is a series of concentric circles of community, complementary not contradictory – at least when viewed in the light of a Christian understanding of citizenship. That understanding, as I suggested earlier, is a 'bifocal' one, with two fields of vision. One is 'near and now', while the other is long-range; one is where we are, the other is where we are heading. It is all too easy to become totally absorbed in the first and lose sight of the second. We must resist that temptation.

There is one more community in which, Christ tells us, we are called to participate, which enfolds all others and is the only one in which we ultimately belong. This is what St Paul refers to in his Letter to the Philippians as 'our commonwealth ... in heaven'. This is St Augustine's 'City of God'. 'Thou hast made us for thyself,' Augustine wrote in his *Confessions*, 'and our hearts are restless until they rest in thee.' Of course, I realize that there are those who struggle to believe in that glorious city and that heavenly community. Nonetheless, regardless of differences in belief or tradition, I suspect that many would agree with me that we as a society are yearning, aching, for an experience of the transcendent, the mystical, the 'more perfect' world to come.

Cilla Black, that famous daughter of Liverpool, was once asked, 'Do you believe in God?' She is said to have replied, 'Well, there must be something greater than the London Palladium!'

Indeed, yes! For Christians, all earthly forms of citizenship are merely rehearsals for that something greater, that perfect community in heaven. As we seek to make sense of this life together, I believe the values of the next can enrich us all and help to make us better citizens, now and for the future.

THE COMMON GOOD

Vincent Nichols

16 MARCH 2000

The Most Revd Vincent Nichols was appointed Archbishop of Birmingham in 2000. He was previously an Auxiliary Bishop of Westminster.

I am grateful for this opportunity to reflect on what the Christian faith has to say about the idea of 'citizenship' in today's society. I do that, of course, from a Catholic perspective. I believe that being a member of the Church has a great deal to contribute to our understanding of citizenship, just as Catholic social teaching in particular has something useful to contribute to our understanding of society and the part each one has to play in it.

It is remarkable that the whole topic of citizenship should have gathered such momentum in the last few years, both in this country and elsewhere, and it is perhaps worth asking why. At least part of the answer, I think, must be because of a fear shared by many people that the cement holding the institutions of our society together has been gradually crumbling and is now in urgent need of repair and renewal. Many of our public institutions – Parliament, the law, the police, the press, and the churches – have seen public confidence in them diminish somewhat over the last decade or more. Various political and social trends point to a diminished active participation in political parties and lower turnouts for elections, especially local ones.

Questions have been raised about whether young people are leaving school with sufficient knowledge about the civil and legal basis of our social life, and the importance of community involvement and the voluntary sector.

There are deeper anxieties, too, about cultural shifts leading to a greater sense of disengagement of individuals from society and the State. Coupled with this are the fears surrounding the yawning gap between the haves and the have-nots in Britain today – with, on the one hand, the wealthy increasingly opting out of state provision in health and education and, on the other hand, too many families and children growing up in poverty, which produces young people who feel they have no stake in society.

Even if some of these fears have been overstated, they are nonetheless real, and rightly should concern us all. It is therefore surely to be welcomed that much attention is being given to the cultivation of active citizenship, for instance through education for citizenship and the teaching of democracy in schools, and the initiatives recently announced by Gordon Brown to help strengthen the voluntary sector.

The 1990 report of the Speaker's Commission on Citizenship, which was established by the last Conservative Government, stated, 'Citizenship, whatever it means, is a cultural achievement, a gift of history, which can be lost or destroyed. The challenge to our society is to create conditions where all who wish can become actively involved, can understand and participate, can influence, persuade, campaign and whistle blow, and in the making of decisions can work together for the mutual good.' The report noted that defining citizenship was not easy, because to do so raises wider ideological and moral questions about the nature of the good society. It quoted the work of T.H. Marshall, who saw citizenship as a developing institution moving towards an ideal. He envisaged the rights of citizenship as involving three elements – civil, political and social – which he argued had developed in Britain over the last three centuries. He said, 'Citizenship requires a direct sense of community based on loyalty to a civilization which is a common possession.'

It seems to me that this notion of an *ideal* is crucial. If citizenship is to be promoted we need, as Marshall said, 'some image of an ideal citizenship against which achievement can be directed'. In other words, we need a vision that helps us to answer two questions: 'What kind of citizens do we want to aspire to be?' and 'What kind of society do we want to create?'

Looked at from the point of view of Christian tradition and teaching, these questions raise again, in a fresh and contemporary way, the relationship between the life of the Church and the life of society. They touch on that complex yet compelling scriptural notion of the 'Kingdom of God'. This kingdom is, as you will understand, inaugurated in Christ, God's truth for all mankind, yet not fully realized until the end of time. The Church is to be found in between the victory of Christ, the 'now', the 'already' of the work of the Spirit in Christ, and the 'not yet' of the reality of this world. We pray, 'Thy kingdom come.' We work for a society which is marked by the justice, peace, truth, love and harmony of that kingdom. Furthermore, in faith we recognize in the Church a certain sign or sacrament of that kingdom, for in its prayer, sacraments and teaching it is a privileged place of the work of the Holy Spirit. In the words of *Lumen Gentium*, the Church is 'given that mission of announcing and establishing in every people the kingdom of Christ and of God and of being on earth the seed and beginning of the kingdom' (*LG* 5).

So it is that the joys and hopes of the society of which each Catholic is a part are his or her joys and hopes also. Progress by society towards the qualities of life of the kingdom are the concern of every member of the Church. That is part of our striving as followers of the Lord. As *Gaudium et Spes* stated, 'Therefore, although we must carefully distinguish earthly progress from an increase in the Kingdom of Christ, such progress is of vital concern for the Kingdom of God, in so far as it can better order human society' (*GS* 39). The task of the

Christian, then, is 'to proclaim aloud both the virtues of the kingdom of God here and now and the hope of the blessed life to come' (*LG* 5). The contribution that a member of the Church wishes to make to society, the manner of being a citizen, will therefore follow from their discipleship of Christ as Lord and from their membership of the Church.

Just this weekend, we have seen a strikingly clear example of what I am struggling to express. Last Sunday, the first Sunday of Lent, was held by the Church in Rome as a 'Day of Pardon' – a day for seeking pardon. A unique liturgy took place in St Peter's Basilica in which, in the words of the official document, 'the Holy Father, in a primatial act as "the one who presides over the churches in charity", and in the name of the whole Church, confessed to the Lord, the God of mercy and compassion, the sins committed in the past and in the present'.

An ancient crucifix was set up in St Peter's. As each moment of the confession took place, lamps were lit before the crucifix. Pardon was asked for many aspects of the life of the Church in these and similar words:

- for our failures 'to walk the way of authentic conversion';
- for 'the contempt and hostility, even to the point of persecution, that some of your children showed against the children of Israel';
- for the sins 'that have harmed the unity of Christ's Body the Church';
- that 'at certain times in history, in the belief that we were serving the faith and the truth, the sons and daughters of the Church yielded to sentiments of intolerance and committed acts of violence against their brothers and sisters who professed other religious beliefs';
- and finally, 'For the role that each one of us has had, with his or her behaviour, in these evils, contributing to a disfigurement of the face of the Church, we humbly ask forgiveness.'

The liturgy was an important culmination of a theme of thought and action that has characterized the recent years of the papacy of Pope John Paul II. In *Tertio Millennio Adveniente*, the Pope invited Christians to undertake a 'purification of memory' and 'to acknowledge before God and before those offended by their actions ... doing so without seeking anything in return, but strengthened only by the love of God which has been poured into our hearts' (No. 33).

This theme and pattern of confession of fault has not been without its critics. Some have been upset because they say that such actions play into the hands of those who wish to belittle the Church, undermining the teaching authority of the Church. Others raise questions about how a person today, even if that person is the Pope, can take responsibility for things that were done in the past. Surely the past is over and done with, none of our concern.

Careful preparation paved the way for that historic ceremony. First of all, the links between past and present have to be made clear. The Church is the Body of Christ. As such, the Church is one in both time and space. The unity of the Church is the unity of Christ, effected through the power of the Holy Spirit. In this unity, the Church includes not only the saints of all ages – those we appeal to in our prayers – but also the sins of all time. In the words of the preparatory document:

> Indeed, in the grace and in the woundedness of sin, the baptized people of today are close to, and in solidarity with, those of yesterday, before the Eternal God. For this reason it can be said that the Church – one in time and space in Christ and in the Spirit – is truly 'at the same time holy and ever in need of purification' (*LG* 8). The Church is able to take on the gifts, the merits and the faults of her children of yesterday and today ... She cannot fail to be wounded by the sins of her children today and yesterday.

Here, then, is a vision of the Church as a society whose bonds reach beyond the confines of time. For the Church it is not possible, nor desirable, to let go of the past, to let go of the dead, for we know that we continue to share the one life of Christ with those who have gone before us, and we look forward to a new and everlasting union with them in the fullness of God.

Is it possible, though, to carry now the responsibilities of the sins of the past? Certainly we carry the consequences of past wrongs. Our own family histories make that clear, as do the social histories of many societies and peoples. Memories are long, and wounds continue to ache long after they have been inflicted, drawing into the circle of consequence many who had no direct part in the original offences. The preparatory work for the papal confession also tried to tackle this question. It states:

> On the level of morality, the request for forgiveness always presupposes an admission of responsibility, precisely the responsibility for a wrong committed against others. Such responsibility may be objective or subjective. Objective responsibility refers to the moral value of the act in itself, in so far as it is good or evil. Subjective responsibility concerns the effective perception by the individual conscience of the goodness or evil of the act that has been done. Subjective responsibility ceases with the death of the one who performed the act. The only responsibility capable of continuing in history can be the objective kind.

The study goes on to reflect that this objective responsibility can be sensed in the burden that weighs so heavily on the conscience of a people, a place, or a time as to constitute 'a kind of moral and religious memory of the evil done'. This common memory gives an eloquent witness to the bonds or links objectively existing between those who committed the evil in the past and their heirs in the present. 'It then becomes possible to speak of objective common responsibility, liberation from which comes, above all, through imploring God's forgiveness for the wrongs of the past,' and through the search for the 'purification of memories'. These have been the steps taken by the Pope, on behalf of the Church.

It seems to me, however, that this ceremony illustrates most vividly some of the qualities that a member of the Church could bring to society through his or her active citizenship. After all, the Church's search for the Kingdom of God, of which it is to be a sign, must have sharp relevance for the development in society of those same qualities.

In political debate today, there seems to be an increasing tension between those who uphold, rigorously, a secular approach to shared public life and those who, on the basis of faith in God, insist on the reality of the sacred immersed within the realities of this world. Differences between these two approaches easily come to mind, but let me highlight two of them, as illustrated by Lord Griffiths in a recent lecture.

Firstly, he pointed out that today there are those who explain the behaviour and meaning of the human person 'primarily, if not entirely, by environment of language, family, upbringing, schooling, class and community. By extending democracy, improving education, pursuing inclusiveness, reforming welfare and creating the cosmopolitan society, individuals can be changed. This is a world of fundamentally good people which cannot make sense of the notion of evil.'

Secondly, he pointed out that hand in hand with this approach to the individual can go a disregard or a lack of a sense of history. It is as if, in an extreme form, we can be brought to some sense of a 'year zero' in which all can begin again, with a reconstruction of society from 'some box of brightly coloured shapes that are to be pieced together'. The past loses its value. 'All that really matters is the present and the future, driven by the pace of change represented in the rise of globalization, secularization and individualism.' To a society and public life at present tempted in both these ways, the Christian citizen will bring the example and symbolism of the papal act of penitence.

Individuals are indeed good, and of course we must strive for reform and inclusiveness. Yet we must also take seriously our in-built propensity for selfishness and neglect of others. The freedom of the individual and the moral responsibility of each person must be understood and nurtured, within a moral framework explored and accepted communally. In this search for shared moral values, the past has as much to offer as the present and the future. The fruit of human wisdom, the response of people of previous generations to the prompting and revelation of God, are crucial parts of the task that we face today.

Similarly, the moral failures of the past have to be acknowledged, not simply so as to clear the way for improved efficiency or future success, but as an act of maturity and responsibility. Often this is difficult in the extreme. It is so for the Church. It is so for a local political party. It is so for a family or a local community. Such a step probably only makes sense in the context of faith in God, who alone knows the hearts of each one of us and who alone can exercise that judgement in justice and love in which lies our freedom.

Citizenship, for the Christian, will entail all these dimensions. How they will be expressed in practice is dependent on the circumstances of each time and place. Nevertheless, this sense of moral responsibility and of moral continuity and linkage to the past is an important aspect of what can be brought to civic life today.

Aspects of this theme have, of course, been recently explored on Merseyside with a reconsideration of the part played in the history of the great city of Liverpool by the slave trade. Careful historical study and a sense of an 'objective common responsibility' have led to public recognition and statements of the evils of the past in the sincere hope of deepening social harmony today.

Anyone familiar with the social teaching of the Church will have spotted in this theme a rather original application of the concept of solidarity. Solidarity is one of those key notions of the social teaching of the Church by which the citizen of today is offered the principles of a moral framework to guide and shape thought and action. But what is its historical context?

There was a particular development of this teaching towards the end of the nineteenth century, when European nations were trying to come to terms with the tremendous social upheavals caused by rapid industrialization. The Church recognized two ideologies locked in conflict – capitalism and Marxist communism – and saw that, as someone put it, 'in capitalism man exploits man and in communism it's the other way round'. The Church objected to both systems for imposing a false, materialist and rigid economic system that denied human dignity and led to great suffering and exploitation.

In a series of papal documents since 1891, successive Popes have endeavoured to reflect on how emerging modern societies function and what principles should guide them if they are to serve the human person. The present Pope has emphasized that at the heart of this teaching is 'the need for conversion to one's neighbour, at the level of the community as well as of the individual'. It is a reorientation that affects each person's relationship with neighbours, communities and the natural environment. It also places the human dignity of all at centre stage, recognizing that this dignity consists in each person being made free by God – free, that is, for a purpose. Society, therefore, should respect human freedom by enabling women and men to take responsibility for their own lives and to co-operate in pursuit of the common good.

This teaching does not, of course, offer a detailed blueprint for society, still less a specific political programme. What this teaching has now developed, however, is a set of consistent and complementary principles, which many people of other faiths or none have also found helpful. There are three of these, and they each have something to add to my reflections on citizenship. The three principles are: the common good, solidarity, and subsidiarity.

First of all, there is the principle of the common good. At one extreme there is a view of society which sees it as no more than a space within which we each pursue our own good in our own way. Society is like a shared student house in which everyone has his or her own room, but no one bothers about the landing, the kitchen or the roof. In this view, other people are by and large incidental to the achievement of my own aims and goals. At the other extreme there is the collectivist vision in which the good of the individual is totally subordinated to the greater good of the State. The individual person is not that important.

The idea of the common good in Catholic social teaching offers something in between (I hesitate to use the phrase 'third way'). Essentially, the common good is the whole network of social conditions that enable all individuals and groups of people to live a full and genuinely human life. It implies that everyone has both a duty to share in promoting the welfare of the community as a whole, and a right to benefit from that welfare. It rejects the idea that any individuals can live fulfilled lives without any thought or concern for others. Without setting out a detailed blueprint of specific policies, the idea of the common good offers us a basic and guiding orientation. Let me quote from the document called *The Common Good* which the Catholic bishops in this country produced in 1997:

> 'Common' implies 'all-inclusive': the common good cannot exclude or exempt any section of the population. If any section of the population is in fact excluded from participation in the life of the community, then that is a contradiction of the concept of the common good and calls for rectification ... A society with insufficient regard for the common good would be unpleasant and dangerous to live in, as well as unjust to those it excluded.

The idea of the common good provides a moral basis for encouraging active citizenship, understood as the cultivation of a wider and deeper engagement of people with the betterment of social conditions, based on a certain vision of what it is to be a human being. That is a vision which denies that we are atomized individuals – rather we are spiritual and moral beings for whom relationships with others are a fundamental part of who we are.

This is underpinned by the second principle, solidarity. The present Pope defines this as 'not a feeling of vague compassion or shallow distress at the misfortunes of so many people, both near and far. On the contrary, it is a firm and persevering determination to commit oneself to the common good; that is to say to the good of all and of each individual, because we are all really responsible for all' (*Solicitudo Rei Socialis*, No. 38). True solidarity arises when we recognize that all human persons are interdependent both with one another and with the rest of creation. The recent action by the Holy Father has given this notion of solidarity a new dimension: our solidarity in moral responsibility across the ages.

'Solidarity' is the Christian word for citizenship. It embodies the moral truth that 'no man is an island, entire of itself'. It helps us to acknowledge the truth that we are all interdependent, and that each person is another 'self' with just the same rights as we claim for ourselves. The moral sense of solidarity enables us to change our motivation, to begin to move away from seeing ourselves as the centre of our world, and to embrace a larger universe of meaning in which we are but one among many, each with a unique value and place.

Listening recently to Lord Alton speaking about successful programmes promoting active citizenship in schools and among young people, I felt that it was not so difficult to put flesh on the statement that solidarity is the Christian name for citizenship. The projects of which he spoke are a great source of encouragement and, I know, of inspiration among teachers. They recognize both the need and the potential in young people to become actively involved in the life of the wider world around them.

The third principle of this teaching is subsidiarity. Here, too, the best definition is given in a papal document, this time by Pius XI in 1931:

> Just as it is gravely wrong to take from individuals what they can accomplish by their own initiative and industry and give it to the community, so also it is an injustice and at the same time a grave evil and disturbance of right order to assign to a greater or higher association what lesser and subordinate organizations can do. For every social activity ought of its very nature to furnish help to the members of the body social, and never destroy or absorb them.

This principle reminds us, and every citizen, that all the functions of civic bodies should always be subsidiary – i.e. directed to helping people realize their destiny by assuming responsibility for their own lives. Basic needs have to be met, and often by the larger, wider bodies, but government should always have only a limited role.

In Europe subsidiarity has gained a wider currency for the proper level at which decisions should be made. In Great Britain, too, we have now embarked upon a new constitutional realignment that could greatly enhance local autonomy. Devolution in Scotland and Wales, the advent of directly elected mayors in England, and the prospect in future years of more powers being devolved to regions in England: all these will dramatically affect the climate of local politics and should help to stimulate greater participation. If all works well, this is indeed subsidiarity in action.

In a few days' time, a document will be issued in London, prepared by Christians and welcomed and supported by London Church leaders, setting out facts and figures about life in London today and raising key questions. It is our attempt to contribute to the shaping of London's future. It will be followed, on 2 April, by a major gathering in St Paul's Cathedral at which the candidates for the position of Mayor of London will respond to the questions of those present. We hope that the cathedral will be full: 2,000 Christians showing their concern about the future of their city and making their views known.

This principle of subsidiarity also helps us to recognize why the place of voluntary work and voluntary organizations is so important. These provide some of the main ways in which people come together to foster the wellbeing of others and to shape their own destiny. Often, through participation in voluntary associations, people realize together the potential and power they can have by taking up responsibility. Movements such as Broad-Based Organizing, and its national training institute, the Citizen Organizing Foundation, have met with great success in bringing together a whole range of people from different faiths and backgrounds. One of its early successes was in Liverpool, in Toxteth. More recently, a successful project has been opened in East London, working on special local political initiatives for the improvement of the neighbourhood. Many of the parishes in East London, as in Liverpool, have found the experience exciting and affirming of what ordinary people can achieve together as citizens in a community.

These and other similar initiatives (and I think of one in North London in which the parish community bought out a next-door strip club and transformed it into their local community centre, a project which took great perseverance but which has immeasurably improved the neighbourhood) are particularly important in a culture which has, for some, induced a sense of passive dependency and which sometimes seems to encourage individuals to see themselves as victims. I do not wish to belittle the genuine suffering of those who are victims, especially of violent crime. Rather, what I have in mind is a social attitude that denies the dignity of the individual by always seeking to shift the burden of responsibility on to others. The broad-based community organizations all have what they call an 'iron rule': never do for others what they can do for themselves. Instead they encourage and enable people to take up responsibility and promote development themselves, in carefully focused and successful steps.

Chancellor Gordon Brown recently emphasized the importance of this voluntary sector. He quoted some interesting figures: every month, 22 million men and women give of their time in voluntary work; every year, half the adult population undertakes some voluntary work – although he noted that it is less popular among the young. He went on to list the strengths of voluntary action:

- It is local and not remote.
- It has the ability to innovate where the State can be inflexible.
- It is personal rather than institutional.
- It fosters a deeper sense of belonging to a wider community.

He also spoke of the need for a new partnership: 'The way forward is not either a constant war of attrition to decide the proper demarcation between charities and government, as if the success of government meant less charity and the success of charity meant less government ... the way forward is a recognition that the voluntary sector is not a cut-price alternative to statutory provision, nor a way of ducking the responsibilities of families, including the extended family.'

He might have added here another temptation or problem: that of how to sustain the spirit and motivation of a voluntary organization while also attaining adequate standards of service and accountability. The 'professionalizing' of a voluntary service, including as it does laudable aims, sometimes loses the very qualities that made it personal, flexible and local. At times the very heart of a local effort is destroyed and the volunteers who were initially most enthusiastic return home disappointed and deprived of the point of active citizenship. The ways in which public funding is channelled to voluntary organizations need to be sensitive to these risks.

We in the Church can be rightly proud of the way in which voluntary work is fostered and sustained in our communities today by the practice of the faith and the desire to express it in practice. Major societies in the life of the Church make a marvellous contribution to the wellbeing of our common life. I hope that, as the practice and encouragement of citizenship goes forward, these societies will continue to prosper.

Most, if not all, of what I have said so far has been to do with the actions of the citizen, understood from the perspective of the Christian faith. I have tried to reflect on what would be the concerns and activities of the citizen who draws strength and motivation from the Church, and from the teaching and example offered by the community of faith. There is, of course, another dimension to the whole topic of citizenship which I have not touched, yet it is a crucial and current topic. To what extent is citizenship not so much a matter of activity as a matter of identity? Does citizenship tell us who we are? Does it resolve the complex questions of national identity?

In some countries this would appear to be so. Citizenship is readily available, whatever a person's ethnic background or parenthood, on the basis of a formal undertaking to accept the responsibilities and duties of that society. In other countries citizenship is much more tied to the identity that a person has been bequeathed by nature or history. In Europe today there are various initiatives aimed at constructing a European identity and a citizenship which could go with it. Not surprisingly, they are controversial!

Here again, the eyes of faith open up for us a further perspective. More than anything else, the disciples of Jesus know that they are citizens of heaven. We have 'another country' to which we belong, and our hearts are set there, too. As the Letter to the Hebrews states:

> Jesus suffered outside the city gate to sanctify his people by his own blood. Let us then go to him, outside the camp, and bear the abuse he endured. For here we have no lasting city but we are looking for the city that is to come. Through him, then, let us continually offer a sacrifice of praise to God, that is, the fruit of lips that confess his name. But do not neglect to do good and to share what you have, for such sacrifices are pleasing to God.
>
> (Hebrews 13:12–16)

This apparent conflict of identities, of citizenship, has been carried by Christians since the first days of the faith. They have continually faced charges of disloyalty to the State or treason against it. They have paid with life and limb, wealth and reputation. The tension will not go away. For, while every Christian is undoubtedly called upon not only to submit to civil authorities in all matters that do not offend conscience, but also to play a vigorous and active part in building up the common life and common good of society, there will always be another appeal, another love, another source of hope.

When these are held together in a tension which is balanced, then the fruit is a profound commitment to the good of society and a selflessness in the service of the common good. When that balance is seriously disrupted, however, then the disciple of the Lord will know where his or her most profound duty lies. Sometimes clashes and breaks are inevitable. They come about, sometimes, on the rock of a moral principle; sometimes, though less often today, on a truth of faith. So we strive to live with a dual citizenship, knowing that so often the aims of both cities are shared, but aware also that at times they part. It is true to say, however, and I hope I have illustrated it to be so, that the faithful disciple of Christ will bring a great deal to our society today, and a great deal that is needed and appreciated by many of our fellow citizens.

WILLIAM ROSCOE:
A CASE STUDY IN CITIZENSHIP

Magnus Magnusson

6 JUNE 2000

Magnus Magnusson KBE is a writer and broadcaster with special interests in Iceland and Scotland, and is a great admirer of William Roscoe.

Two summers ago, in 1998, I was invited to deliver the annual Roscoe Memorial Lecture. This time I am here at the invitation of the Foundation for Citizenship – and who could refuse an invitation from an organization whose headquarters are at such an appropriate address: Roscoe Court? But there was another invitation, penned by Roscoe himself in 1802 and first published in the *Gentleman's Magazine* in 1806. It was an invitation to a ball – the Butterfly's Ball:

> Come take up your hats, and away let us haste
> To the Butterfly's Ball and the Grasshopper's Feast.
> The trumpeter Gadfly has summoned the crew,
> And the revels are now only waiting for you.

How could I refuse? So this morning I made haste to the Roscoe Infants School in Alison Road, which proudly boasts a Roscoe Butterfly Garden. The area of the garden was originally allotments for the surrounding council houses until it was handed over to the school in 1981 – the 150th anniversary of Roscoe's death from 'flu in 1831. The patch of ground was landscaped and planted with suitable shrubs and flowers like buddleia to attract butterflies. It is an environmental garden in the best sense, in that it surrounds an 'outdoor classroom' area where children can practise all manner of skills – writing and listing wildlife names, counting creatures, learning about simple biology, about presentation, about thinking.

I found it entrancing. It is a dark, secret, heavily canopied wooded area, like the wildwood of Kenneth Grahame's *Wind in the Willows*. Like old Badger, I felt very much at home there, and so did the youngsters who showed it to me in the pouring rain. They pointed out the bird box they had put up for nesting bluetits and showed me the pond where they could go pond-dipping. The garden and its butterflies have left their mark on the school: the school badge was changed, in fact, to feature a butterfly. Afterwards the youngsters told me about William Roscoe – that he had been an MP, that he had been a banker and, above all, that he had been against making people slaves. It was very touching. Roscoe's memory is in good young hands.

Later, I had the honour of meeting William Roscoe, citizen of this great city – in spirit, at least. There he was, larger than life, superintending the main staircase of the Walker Art Gallery here in Liverpool, glowering across at Napoleon.

Finally, a funny thing happened to me on my way to St George's Hall. I met William Roscoe in the flesh. You may not believe this, but the name of the taxi driver was indeed William Roscoe. I do not know – nor does he, yet – whether or not he is a direct descendant of *our* William Roscoe, but I'll bet my bottom dollar that an army of archivists will be mobilized to find out.

Before I came here two years ago for the annual Roscoe Memorial Lecture, I had only a very vague idea of who William Roscoe was. I had to start from scratch, to find Roscoe for myself, and that, to me, is always the best part of a task. I love researching. I love finding things out for their own sake. In that respect I can proudly claim to be an 'opsimath', which simply means 'one who keeps on learning late in life'.

I was looking for a man who was an opsimath himself. Roscoe was a man who was always thirsting for knowledge on a variety of subjects – on art and agriculture, botany and horticulture, history and literature, philosophy and politics. He was an enigmatic, energetic, idealistic visionary – a man *of* his time who was also *ahead* of his time, a true citizen of Liverpool at the time when the town was starting a period of rapid expansion from a fledgling port to a major commercial metropolis.

There is nothing more enjoyable than doing your research in the field. I went on a personal pilgrimage, to try to make contact with the spirit of Roscoe if I could. But I have to confess that looking for overt traces of Roscoe in Liverpool in those days – apart from a few lingering place names – was not an easy quest. The public memory of Roscoe seemed to be fading in the city he helped to make so great.

My first call was to where he was buried on 5 July 1831, at the former Unitarian Chapel in Renshaw Street. The church was demolished a long time ago and replaced by Central Hall, but the cemetery behind it, facing on to Mount Pleasant, was made into what is listed in Terry Cavanagh's book on *Public Sculpture of Liverpool* as 'Roscoe Garden'. It turned out to be a rather small walled area opposite the multistorey car park in Mount Pleasant, between the Pit-stop Garage and a pub called the Compass Inn. It lay behind railings, with nothing to indicate what it was, and the gate was padlocked. It occurred to me to make enquiries at the nearby Mount Pleasant Hotel and, *mirabile dictu*, the receptionist just happened to have a key to it, although she had no idea of its significance.

Inside the tiny garden there is a Doric octagonal memorial, inscribed with the names of some of those who had been buried there – including William Roscoe. It is not much of a shrine, I have to say. When I went into the garden it was all rather doleful. The memorial itself is decaying, the bronze memorial plaques are in poor condition and almost illegible. It was all rather seedy and dilapidated, in fact.

Farther up Mount Pleasant, at the junction with Hope Street, I visited the area where Roscoe was born in March 1753 in a pub called the Old Bowling Green Tavern. I do not know exactly where it was in Hope Street. What I found was a convent, the administrative building of John Moores University, and a theatre which started as a revivalist hall exactly 100 years after Roscoe's birth and which showed the very first movies in Liverpool in 1896 – The Everyman.

Roscoe's dad was Mine Host of the Old Bowling Green Tavern, but he also kept a market garden nearby – a pretty big place, several acres in fact – where he grew vegetables and early potatoes. Young William worked hard in the garden, digging and delving, helping the family to earn its livelihood. We know from his letters that he took much pleasure in that – indeed, towards the end of his life he wrote to an old friend, 'If I were now asked whom I consider to be the happiest of the human race, I should answer, those who cultivate the earth by their own hands.' A touch of Voltaire's *Candide* there: after all his picaresque adventures, Candide's final comment was, '*Il faut cultiver notre jardin*' – 'We must cultivate our garden.'

It was these boyhood experiences, quite clearly, which helped to make him one of the foremost botanists of his day. To pursue *that* line of enquiry, I went to the home which was Roscoe's favourite residence during his years of prosperity. He bought it in 1799, a seat of elegant hospitality and refined learning where he was best able to indulge his botanical interests: Allerton Hall, just outside the town then, a spacious, sandstone mansion set in '150 acres of lawns, gardens, pleasure grounds, plantations and desmesne lands', where he lived until he went bankrupt and had to sell it in 1816.

I discovered that it is now a hostelry called the Pub on the Park – so where better to enjoy a pilgrim's lunch? One room of the house is said to be haunted but, alas, there is no sign of the shade of Roscoe there now. The building was devastated by fire not so long ago and its interior has been completely rebuilt at considerable expense. There was no blue plaque to indicate that it was once the home of William Roscoe; there was no information sheet about Roscoe available to patrons. It had no resonance, no sense of the great man's presence. I felt oddly cheated, because there is such a great story to be told. I am delighted to hear that the Area Environmental Officer has now planted a nectar border behind Allerton Hall to encourage butterflies to come and have a ball.

You can tell a man by the sort of people he admires. In Roscoe's case, the man he admired above all others was Lorenzo de' Medici, Lorenzo the Magnificent, the fifteenth-century Florentine ruler and patron of the arts who transformed Florence into the leading state of Renaissance Europe, both politically and artistically. He was a distinguished lyric poet as well as being, in the words of Niccolò Machiavelli, 'the greatest patron of literature and art that any prince has ever been'.

This was the man about whom Roscoe decided to write a lavish biography. It was a huge undertaking and took him many years to write. It was also a huge success and earned him a towering international reputation as a scholar, biographer and historian. After its first publication, in two volumes, in 1796 it ran to seven editions during Roscoe's lifetime, and another five after his death – the fifth, edited by William Hazlitt in 1883, came out 87 years after the first edition. All this from a man who had no formal education after the age of 11!

There is no doubt in my mind that Roscoe saw his own role as being cast in the mould of the great Lorenzo – or, at least, that he relished and cultivated the similarities between them. Like Lorenzo, Roscoe became a patron of the arts, a scholar of international repute, a banker (although his bank crashed after the end of the Napoleonic Wars), and a politician for a short time. He and his friends created the Liverpool Athenaeum (a scholars' library which opened in 1799). They founded the

Royal Institution, which later became the University of Liverpool. With two other businessmen, Roscoe also founded the
Mechanics' and Apprentices' Library in 1823, which eventually
became Liverpool Polytechnic and finally John Moores University. In 1998 the JMU celebrated the 175th anniversary of the
original foundation by William Roscoe. As an early Liverpool
historian, James Picton, put it, 'No resident of Liverpool has
done more to elevate the character of the community, by uniting
the successful pursuit of literature and art with the ordinary
duties of the citizen and man of business.'

Above all, like Lorenzo, William Roscoe was a 'Renaissance
man', a 'world citizen'. His concerns were not only for his fellow
citizens of Liverpool, but also for the citizens of the wider world.
Nothing shows this more clearly than his lifelong support of the
abolition of slavery. He won election to Parliament in 1807, on
the eve of the Abolition of Slavery Bill that year. In the debate in
the House of Commons he announced proudly, 'I have long
resided in the town of Liverpool. For 30 years I have never
ceased to condemn this inhuman traffic; and I consider it the
greatest happiness of my existence to lift up my voice, on this
occasion, against it.'

It was not the most popular position for a Liverpool MP to
advocate. The Liverpool of his day was at the very heart of the
slave trade. By the middle of the eighteenth century, Liverpool
merchants were handling five-eighths of the English slave trade
and three-sevenths of the slave trade in Europe. It was a huge
business, generating about £17 million in 1807 alone. A thousand Liverpool ship's captains were involved – including John
Newton, who later renounced the trade and wrote the hymn
'Amazing Grace'.

Roscoe's principled objection to this evil commerce was to
cost him dear. When he returned to Liverpool he was met by a
mob of infuriated slave-traders and seamen who attacked the
coach in which he was travelling. They pulled him from the
carriage and assaulted him. As well as the personal humiliation

and discomfort of this attack, it was also to cost Roscoe his seat in Parliament after only three months. But that was not as important to him as making what he passionately believed to be a just and humane stand on a complex moral, ethical and political issue. Roscoe was also an advocate of penal reform, demanding less severity. The purpose of prison and the aim of punishment should be not retribution but rehabilitation, he said – an idea far ahead of his time.

Roscoe was also a man of the classical Augustan age in Britain, the century of Alexander Pope and Capability Brown, when poetry as well as parkland enjoyed a heyday of manicured formality. At Allerton Hall Roscoe was able to enjoy the cultivation of his extensive formal garden. He could also give more time here to the proper study of botany, and this was perhaps his most profound and enduring love. As he was to write in the prospectus for the Botanic Garden in Liverpool, 'Even the cultivation of the fine arts, however alluring in its progress, must yield to the superiority of the study of nature; for who will venture to compare the productions of the painter and sculptor with the original?'

Roscoe was a very serious botanist indeed, an 'applied ecologist' rather than an academic, a pioneer at a time when botany as a scientific subject was still in its infancy. Botanic gardens for the cultivation and scientific study of plants had been established in Italy, Switzerland, France and Germany. In Britain, Oxford, Edinburgh and Chelsea had been established in the seventeenth century, while Kew was still merely a royal park. It was typical of Roscoe's visionary ambitions for his town that he wanted to ensure that Liverpool, too, should have a botanic garden.

With a few friends of like mind, he prepared a prospectus in the hope of raising sufficient money by subscription and allotting shares. The appeal succeeded, and in 1803 the Botanic Garden was opened on a 10-acre plot on a hill top, then outside the town, in what is now the part of the city bounded by Myrtle Street, Melville Place and Olive Street, next door to Liverpool University.

Soon the Botanic Gardens boasted a fine herbarium, a library and a conservatory with five heated sections capable of growing plants from any part of the world. By 1808 it housed more than a thousand species of plants, shrubs and trees. There were evening functions for the social elite of Liverpool to stroll through the grounds, discreetly serenaded by an unobtrusive band.

So what happened to it? When I went in search of it, there was no trace of the garden. All I found was a spanking new housing estate in red brick with comforting names like Melville Grove, Minster Court and Freedom Close. In 1836 the outer part of the site had been sold for development – including, horror of horrors, a prison. The prison never materialized (it was built at Walton instead), but the Botanic Garden was by then clearly under threat and it was moved by the Corporation to a new site at Edge Lane, two miles away, conservatory and all.

So I took my pilgrim's scrip and staff up Botanic Road to the corner of Edge Lane, in the lee of the imposing Littlewoods block, to see what was left of it. I knew that it had flourished for the rest of the century, but had then declined rapidly. A railway marshalling yard and a gasworks made uncongenial neighbours, and it was in a sorry state by November 1940, when the great five-part glasshouse complex was destroyed by German bombs. Mercifully, the library and herbarium had been transferred to safer quarters at the turn of the century.

In 1957 it ceased to be called the Botanic Garden. The name was changed to Wavertree Park. The writing was on the wall. There was a large walled garden adjoining Wavertree Park, but I found no way of getting in. The two gates I came upon were firmly padlocked. At the junction of Botanic Road and Edge Lane there was a building which was originally the park keeper's house, but which was boarded up and silent (and there was plenty of writing on *its* walls). From what I could see through the locked gates, the huge walled garden was still in reasonably good condition, but there was nothing and no one to tell me about the Roscoe connection here.

In 1964 Roscoe's Botanic Garden was moved to its third home, in Harthill and Calderstones Park. My quest was clearly approaching its Grail. I stopped at a block of sandstone bearing a dedicatory inscription commemorating the move: 'In replacement of the Edge Lane Botanic Garden'. Beside it is an imposing glasshouse – but it does not hold plants. It houses the remarkable collection of six Neolithic standing stones covered with spirals and cup-and-ring markings (the original Calder stones from nearby) which had formed a burial site some 5,000 years ago.

This glasshouse, in fact, was the vestibule to Roscoe's translocated Botanic Garden. This is where the residue had come: the great orchid collection, the fernery, the whole living collection of indoor plants, all housed in a tailor-built conservatory. Alas, there was a time in the 1980s when things did not go well for Liverpool, and during that sad decade everything was changed. The orchids and the indoor plants were transferred to Greenhill Nurseries, leaving not a rack behind. Not a rack – but certainly a wreck. Behind that charming vestibule glasshouse there is now dereliction. It seemed to be the ultimate end of Roscoe's magnificent vision.

It is not really the end, however. My guides round Calderstone Park two years ago were two of the Rangers team, Paul Rivera and Ronnie McLaughlin. They both had such an enormous enthusiasm for and commitment to the idea of sharing the wonders of nature with the people of Liverpool that they seemed to me to be the true inheritors of the Roscoe vision. Roscoe would certainly be proud to see how marvellously well they are cherishing his dream today. And it is bearing fruit. Tomorrow, indeed, some of the collection is being planted out in St John's Gardens behind St George's Hall, ready for Liverpool's 'Britain in Bloom' entry. Also this week, other parts of the collection are being transferred to Sefton Park Palm House, which is being restored.

I know that the word 'green' has become a bit threadbare as an automatic label for anything deemed to be environmentally OK, but I do believe that there is a real concept of 'green citizenship' which should be taken into account. The meaning of the word 'citizen' is not confined to 'an inhabitant of a city or a town', even though it is derived from the French word *cité*. It also means a native or inhabitant of any state, nation or place. Similarly, the word 'citizenship' means 'the condition or status of a citizen, with its rights and duties' and 'a person's conduct as a citizen'. I stress the importance of the *duties* as well as the rights of citizenship. That was how Roscoe saw his citizenship of Liverpool – his 'green' citizenship of Liverpool, as I like to call it. He saw no distinction between economy and ecology – after all, both words derive from the same Greek root, the word *oikos*, meaning 'house'. Both economy and ecology are basically about good housekeeping, good husbandry.

So how well have today's citizens built on the intellectual foundations laid by people like Roscoe? I am delighted to see that concern with green issues has been growing dramatically here in recent years. What is happening now is a recognition that social and economic improvement can only come about on a lasting basis if it is rooted in care for the environment: in effect, development has to be sustainable.

This requires the wise use and management of the world's natural resources. It is concerned with respecting environmental quality and natural resources. 'Think globally,' we are enjoined – and that means thinking in terms of global warming, ozone depletion, biodiversity, deforestation and general resource depletion. We are also enjoined to 'think locally', however, and that is where places like Liverpool come into their own, through Local Agenda 21.

Local Agenda 21 springs from a momentous event in global environmental politics, the Earth Summit in 1992 at Rio de Janeiro. The representatives of 179 nations agreed to a declaration comprising 27 principles, all concerned with the need for *sustainable* development. In order to achieve those aims, it was realized that action had to be taken at the grass roots, and that all citizens throughout the world should be able to make a contribution to their own environmental destiny. Hence the concept of Local Agenda 21 – an agenda for the twenty-first century – in which the principles of sustainable development were to be translated into practice at the local level: ways in which ordinary people, inspired by their local authority, can do something about the environment in which they live. Local Agenda 21 provides the opportunity for people to think through the priorities for their own area, to establish Local Biodiversity Action Plans and to influence the direction of change.

Our cities are not really the 'concrete jungles' of popular perception. From the city centres outwards there are extensive areas of green space. Some of them are sterile – the close-cropped deserts of traditional recreation grounds and playing fields; but there is also an abundance of what Chris Baines, the apostle of urban nature, calls 'unofficial *wildspace*'. The mixter-maxter of mineral workings, railway land, demolished factories, old waste tips and neglected allotments adds up to a huge network of wildlife habitat – 'countryside on your doorstep' to the 40 million people in Britain who live and work in towns. It is their only direct contact with wildlife and the natural world.

Liverpool, for example, with its wealth of parks and open spaces, is home to a tremendous variety of wildlife. The city also houses the remnants of old woodlands, like Childwall Woods and Woolton Woods. No fewer than 25 sites have been officially selected as Sites of Nature Conservation Value because of their importance for nature. It is a wonderful litany, a naturalist's paradise if you know where to look. How many people outside Liverpool realize what a wonderful city of nature Liverpool is becoming?

It was this embryo city of nature which William Roscoe hymned in his delightful children's poem, 'The Butterfly's Ball and the Grasshopper's Feast'. Roscoe would be delighted to know that Liverpool itself is home today to more than 20 varieties of butterfly. The grasshopper's feast goes on, although the fare may not be quite as sumptuous as before.

I believe that it is incumbent upon all of us to provide dynamic, living city landscapes which help us to celebrate the seasons, to enjoy the song of birds and the scent of wildflowers, the Butterfly's Ball and the Grasshopper's Feast. Nurturing the urban landscape is essential for our wellbeing and our quality of life. It is important spiritually and culturally – but it also brings more tangible environmental benefits. The citizens of Liverpool today, building on the legacy of their pre-Victorian visionaries, are now just as concerned with the *environmental* development of the city, and have risen magnificently to the challenge of the new century. That, to me, is what good citizenship is ultimately about.

Also, am I being over-optimistic in believing that the tide is turning as far as the memory of William Roscoe is concerned? I do not think so. There is now a Liverpool Heritage Walk which takes in the Old Bowling Green Tavern where Roscoe spent his childhood. He shares pride of place at the stopping point here with John Lennon, who was born not far away in Liverpool Maternity Hospital in 1940.

The little padlocked Roscoe Garden in Mount Pleasant has now been unpadlocked and many people sit there, especially at lunchtime. The grass has been trimmed and it all looks much better cared for than when I was there two years ago.

What about the huge walled garden at Wavertree Park? Well, there seems to have been a transformation there too. There is a spanking new sign in white and deep blue announcing that the name of the place is 'Botanic Park' – that name was new to me. Perhaps on my last visit I was unlucky enough to have come upon the only two gates which were padlocked. The walled garden is now indubitably open to the public. It is a place of abundant but crumbling magnificence: broad boulevards, thumping great rhododendron bushes, clematis climbing wildly all over the place – and dandelions shouldering their thuggish way up everywhere.

In one of the boulevards I came across two seated, headless statues in casual eighteenth-century garb, facing one another across an avenue. I fell upon them with glad cries, despite the fact that one of them was a bit legless (his right leg was missing, to be precise). The inscriptions on the plinths were so worn as to be illegible – but surely one of them must be William Roscoe? And the other perhaps one of his cronies and fellow founders of the Botanic Gardens?

There is nothing like an archivist to knock the stuffing of romance out of you. In a fever of excitement I phoned the archivist in the History section of the Central Library in William Brown Street. She told me that the statues depicted two cronies, right enough – but they were cronies from Robert Burns's wonderful poem, 'Tam o' Shanter', sitting in the pub 'getting glorious' during an epic drinking session: Tam himself and his pal Souter Johnny. In fact there *is* a connection with Roscoe, whether intended or not. Robert Burns was one of the fellow poets Roscoe most admired, and whom he hoped (in vain, as it turned out) to entertain in Liverpool one day.

Finally, last year, in their last formal act of 1999, Liverpool's civic leaders issued a public apology for Liverpool's shameful role at the epicentre of the European slave trade. The 99 members of Liverpool City Council unanimously passed this resolution: 'It is time the city gave expression to its sense of remorse over the effects that the slave trade had on countless millions of people and on the culture of the continent of Africa, the Caribbean and the USA.'

The Council then convened a special extraordinary meeting, with no other business on the agenda, to set up a working party to identify programmes of action which will recognize and respond to the city's multiracial inheritance and celebrate the skills and talents of all its people. One of its proposals is to upgrade the little Roscoe Garden in Mount Pleasant into a Slavery Memorial Garden: cultivating the garden of our history. After all, the year 2007 is the bicentenary of the Abolition of Slavery Act, which Roscoe championed so passionately. It is also the 800th birthday of Liverpool itself. By that year (if not before) the garden in Mount Pleasant will have been transformed into the Slavery Memorial Garden. What could be more appropriate?

It is a far cry from the Toxteth Riots of 1981. It might seem an even further cry from Roscoe and his impassioned opposition to the Liverpool slave trade nearly two centuries ago. Liverpool's unprecedented public apology and act of reconciliation were presented by David Alton to a Slavery Conference in the tiny African republic of Benin, situated on what became known as the Slave Coast. In Benin, the apology was graciously received by the black participants there. The apology, and the Slavery Memorial Garden, would have been seen by William Roscoe as the absolute historical justification of his stance as a humanitarian, a philanthropist, a scholar and a botanist – Liverpool's First Citizen *par excellence.*

CITIZEN VIRTUES
A New Pattern for Living
David Alton

We have never been so materially affluent, and yet modern life seems less and less able to meet our expectations.

Since the death of Diana, Princess of Wales and the landslide victory of New Labour in Britain, a search for fresh values has begun. Tolerance, justice, compassion and community are words used more and more today.

Just what are those values and how can they be practised in schools, homes and workplaces? 'Healthy communities,' writes David Alton, 'are not founded on a mixture of rights, entitlements and individual choice, but need to be balanced by an awareness of civic duties, personal responsibilities and community obligations.'

In *Citizen Virtues* David Alton draws on his considerable experience at the forefront of the fight to bring values back into society. In practical, down-to-earth terms, he spells out how everyone can take part in being responsible, ethical, discerning, confident and active citizens – preserving people's dignity, caring for the environment and working for a more just and humane world. And that world starts in your local neighbourhood.